BECOMING AN UNSTOPPABLE *Woman*

MOMPRENEUR PART II

INSPIRING STORIES AND PRACTICAL ADVICE FOR MOMPRENEURS ON THEIR PATH TO SUCCESS

HANNA OLIVAS & ASHLEY PAKULSKI

ALONG WITH 15 INSPIRING MOMPRENEURS

Table of Contents

INTRODUCTION

In the whirlwind of modern life, being a mom and an entrepreneur can feel like navigating through a maze of challenges. But within these challenges lies immense potential for growth, resilience, and transformation. Welcome to "Becoming an Unstoppable Woman Mompreneur PT 2", where we dive into the journeys of incredible women who have conquered the dual roles of motherhood and entrepreneurship.

Through the pages of this book, you'll encounter stories of perseverance, triumph, and the unwavering spirit of women who refused to let obstacles define them. From the highs of success to the lows of adversity, each story is a testament to the power of resilience and determination.

Join us on this transformative journey as we celebrate the unstoppable spirit of women and empower each other to rise above challenges and embrace our full potential.

Hanna Olivas

Founder & CEO of She Rises Studios

https://www.linkedin.com/company/she-rises-studios/
https://www.facebook.com/sherisesstudios
https://www.instagram.com/sherisesstudios_llc/
www.SheRisesStudios.com

Author, Speaker, and Founder. Hanna was born and raised in Las Vegas, Nevada, and has paved her way to becoming one of the most influential women of 2022. Hanna is the co-founder of She Rises Studios and the founder of the Brave & Beautiful Blood Cancer Foundation. Her journey started in 2017 when she was first diagnosed with Multiple Myeloma, an incurable blood cancer. Now more than ever, her focus is to empower other women to become leaders because The Future is Female. She is currently traveling and speaking publicly to women to educate them on entrepreneurship, leadership, and owning the female power within.

LOVE AND COFFEE ARE MY MAGIC POWER

By Hanna Olivas

All moms have a magical power within. We kiss owies and they go away. We wipe away tears and turn them into wishes come true. We manage to be in two places at one time. We always smile even when we want to cry. We are the first ones to rise and the last to sleep. It seems we have an unending amount of energy— or so our children believe. Being a mother is truly one of the biggest blessings of my life. I have five children ages ten to thirty. Each child is so different and requires a different magical power from me.

For example, my middle and youngest daughters require my patience power. As I sit here writing this, I laugh because it's so true. My oldest son requires me to use my communication magic because he is an onion— it's one layer at a time with him. My middle son requires my sensitivity magic powers because he feels everything. My oldest daughter is my diamond in the rough, and she requires my intuitive magical powers. She keeps everything in. As I describe to you my five children and the magical powers I use, I realize no matter how old they are, they will always want and need their mom and my magic. Mom magic is real!

In addition to raising children, I am a wife and grandmother. I run several successful businesses, and I am a traveler. I absolutely love traveling with my family and experiencing new places and things.

Now that you have a little background on me and some of my magic powers, let me tell you where it all starts. Every day I wake and dash to my sexy coffee machine. I bet you thought I was going to say my husband. Nope! It's coffee. The smell of my first morning cup brings me joy. As I sit and drink the cup of what I believe is magic, I pray, read, and meditate. I love my mornings of gratitude and solitude.

Every mama needs her alone time— end of discussion! After I finish my morning ritual, the siren sounds at approximately 7 AM. This is when we move fast. Get the kids up and ready, pack lunch, drop them off at school, and hope that this time I haven't forgotten anything. As soon as they're off at school, I am off to run my company. It's time for a different magic hat. I have a team of approximately fifteen employees, and each one of them requires a mom superpower. Sometimes—or most times—it's patience and communication. I typically work nine hours a day, five days a week, and I try to do the balancing act most days. But let's be real, this requires skill and talent. I say this because I haven't even begun to discuss my wife magic. Yup, it's a thing. My hubby whom I love dearly also needs love, attention, affection, and a wife who is present, who listens, and gives understanding. One who knows his quirky ways and needs.

How the hell do I manage all this and not lose my shit one hundred times a day? Well, the truth is, I do lose it or have at least one WTF moment a day! I'm not going to pretend any of this is easy because being a mama is like being a warrior at times. I'm often on the battlefield of laundry, dishes, and sticky stuff. When the WTF moments happen, that's when I call my own mama and she uses her magic to calm me. Thank God for moms, right? Who knew having children was like a combo of the George Lopez Show and Family Feud?

Most days, I get through with laughter and coffee. However, there are days when I need to refill my magic cup before it runs out. As a mama, we must always take care of ourselves first. Yup, you heard me! It's not being selfish, so drop the mom-guilt now! Before you can help your children, you must take care of yourself. How and when is up to you! I usually take a mom day on Sundays and do whatever I want. I read, journal, and love a good facial or massage. I also highly recommend yoga because it gives you that inner silence we need most. I make sure my kids, grandkids, and hubby give me the space I need to replenish what I have used.

And yes, hubby gets his alone time too. He goes fishing or golfing often, and even after so many years of marriage, we still "date" each other with a date night or two. There is so much that goes into being a mom, wife, and grandmother. It's never-ending. One of the greatest gifts of being a grandmother is seeing those sweet faces, spoiling them rotten, and returning them to their parents with lots of sugar and loud toys. Payback!

I believe mom magic is real, and it's incredible! To be able to create a tiny little human and watch that human go through life is one of my most cherished things in life. Seeing my youngest to oldest thrive and grow into incredible adults is so amazing. I always say, "Damn, I'm good." I raised my kids to be kind, loving, hard-working, and giving children. My grandkids are the same way.

I am truly blessed beyond measure. Is it all picture-perfect? Nope. Are there days when I've wanted to give up? Yes—but I can't imagine life without them.

My mom magic comes from prayer, faith, unconditional love, and patience that never runs out. My five tips to keep your magic cup full are simple.

1. Pray.
2. Journal.
3. Communicate - because it is key with kids.
4. Self-care.
5. Honesty - when you need help, ask!

Lastly, I would also advise building your mom magic dream team. It truly takes a village to raise your children. So be open to asking for help. That's a power too; it's called vulnerability. Ask your family and friends, church members, your therapist; heck, even your banker! Anyone who is positively vested in your child and their wellbeing. As a mom, never be afraid to ask for help! Remember mamas: progress over perfection. The only perfect mom is a happy mom!

XOXO Hanna

Ashley Pakulski

Ashley Pakulski The Mompreneur Coach
Visibility & Success Coach

https://www.facebook.com/ashleypakulskithemompreneurcoach
https://www.instagram.com/theashleypakulski/
https://linktr.ee/TheMompreneurCoach
https://www.facebook.com/groups/mompreneurssuccesscircle/

Ashley Pakulski, born and raised in Canada, is a dedicated mom, fur baby mom, and passionate advocate for women's empowerment. As The Mompreneur Coach, bestselling author, and team member with She Rises Studios, Ashley has guided many women to step into their power and confidently achieve their goals. Through her own journey of overcoming personal challenges with trauma and addiction, Ashley discovered the transformative power of self-help books and personal development. Diving into inner work and mindset shifts, she harnessed the power of her thoughts and created her Signature Framework. With her warm and relatable approach, Ashley inspires women to embrace their potential, turn their dreams into reality, and make meaningful impacts in their business and lives.

THE ART OF ABUNDANCE

By Ashley Pakulski

"See yourself living in abundance and you will attract it. It always works, it works every time, with every person."
— Bob Proctor

The word abundance can mean something different to each person. This can be an abundance of wealth, love, creativity, gratitude, and so on. What does the word abundance mean to you? This is an important question to ask because this also reflects your mindset towards life, money, success, and so on. Abundance to me is a feeling of love and richness, a lot of opportunities, and a growth mindset. The key to achieving anything you desire is feeling it as you already have it and not having scarcity and lack blocking your success. See, money is energy, and it is a tool we use. But there are many beliefs you can have that are blocking money from coming your way. The richness you desire is all there, right in front of you. I want to share my journey with you and what I do to keep myself open to receiving more abundance (not just about money), even when life can happen and derail me. Let's face it, we aren't always going to have everything go our way. Bumps will happen; big, unexpected things. One thing I have learned is that it's ok to feel it out, but you really truly have to believe and do the work to keep yourself focused and leveled. Your thoughts are so powerful, and everything that you have gone through in your life has been programmed in your subconscious mind. This all affects the actions you take today and how you show up in your business. Your thoughts and beliefs are what are holding you back from receiving the riches you desire. See, I have been on this mindset of mastery journey for many years. I have learned so much and seen the results you can get when you practice these tools. I have also seen how quickly it can go back and forth, from having what you desire to losing it all, to gaining more of what you want, and it's like a cycle. But you need to know how to do the work to make sure you can keep it all instead of losing it. These again go back to your beliefs.

What are your thoughts and beliefs about money? When you go shopping and you are over your budget, what are you thinking or saying to yourself? When you are buying something, do you feel nervous? These are all signs to look at. See, you may be wondering, "Ok, Ashley, why are you talking to me about this?" You might already be aware but remember success is 80% mindset and 20% strategy, of which I think a percentage should be your tribe. Anyway, I want you to go back to your childhood, or even to now, and question what you think about money and write it out on a piece of paper.

- Do you think money comes and goes quickly?
- Do you think it's hard to make money?
- Do you think it's bad to have too much money?

Really think about your relationship with money and how you talk about it with others. Getting crystal clear with your money mindset talk is what is going to be part of your success as a mompreneur. If you think you are not worthy or good enough, you will block yourself from clients coming in and showing up in your business. Trust me. I know how it can affect you and make it seem like you are fighting yourself but you are trying to break free from people's past thoughts or things you heard about money and success. You may seem like the crazy one in your family, talking about big dreams and things you want, and everyone around you is saying, "Well that's just a dream." You are pulling left and right because you know what you want to achieve and help the world but these deep-rooted beliefs are holding you back. When things don't go your way, you start to say, "Maybe they are right."

Let me tell you, they are not right. They are saying this because they are staying in their comfort zone and don't believe in themselves. This isn't a bad thing to say about them because we all have our own fears and doubts. What is important is that you need to break through these beliefs and really believe you can do this. Because you can. You have had little successes, you signed on clients, you went on that family trip, you are living in the home you wanted, and you are taking care of your health, but still there's something inside of you that is making you doubt yourself and your capabilities. We all have them and I will tell you I do too, even as a coach specializing in this. But that is why having tools to help with this can help you push through. This is what I want to share with you but first let me share my money mindset story with you.

Since I was a young child/teen I heard "money stories" from the people close to me, and I have seen some stuff. One side was all about how to make more money doing your own thing and making life look simple by doing the things you love. On the other hand, the other side worked hard for their money. Now, running a business can have its ups and downs, its challenges, and it can definitely burn you out, but you have to know what you are doing. You have to be strategic, AND you have to take out the wheats from the garden. Meaning, your beliefs, doubts, and fears. I have experienced since I was a young child that selling is a bad thing. We make it up in our minds that selling is a bad thing. That's where I was at. I HATED SELLING. I worked at a clothing store and when I went up to the people asking how they were and trying to sell an outfit, I cringed, even if it was asking if they needed help with anything that they were looking for and showing them and selling.

But see, it's not that I just heard people close to me saying, "Oh they are just trying to sell," or "Look why this 'product' WON'T work." Instead of looking at the good of things, it was always about looking at why it won't be good and won't work.

Another thing is that you have stored things in your subconscious since a young age, not just having heard money stories but also things that were said to you that could impact you today without even realizing it. Things like if you were criticized, made fun of, told you can't do something, etc. Your beliefs about the world are formed at such a young age. They are saying now that this happens even as early as while you are in your mother's wound.

You can have people's lingering words programmed in your subconscious questioning your own self-worth, your belief in yourself. This affects every way you show up in your business and it doesn't matter if you are just starting your business or if you are on your way to making your six-figures. See, every level in your business is going to require a newer version of you. Each level you step into will resurface or have beliefs that you need to work through in order to reach your desired level of success. Hear me out. You make more money and then you seem to be back in the same situation you were before. You are stuck on a plateau at the same income level, and no matter what you are doing and trying, you can't reach that next level of success. Well, let me tell you this is the limiting beliefs you have around money and there is something that you need to work through. See, this work isn't that you wave the magic wand and it is fixed overnight. This is ongoing work for life! This is how you fuel yourself for success - by doing the inner and mindset work daily. If you want a fun, easy way that will transform your life, start doing morning and night routines. These are game changers. Grab the first book of "Becoming An Unstoppable Woman Mompreneur." I shared that in there. Plus, there are even more tools and strategies you can use because you will have two complete series.

Let's fast forward and move to the abundance zone. Doing the inner and mindset work, I uncovered and healed many things within myself. It's been a journey, and it's a lifetime journey, as I mentioned before. I am so grateful I taught my daughter these powerful tools because they really do transform your life and mindset and put you in the abundance zone. You have to learn to love money and know money loves you. When tough times happen, don't think, "Maybe people were right," look at the solution, and find the answer to help you through this lesson. There were many times I did not know how I was going to make ends meet or pay a certain bill that was due but putting these tools into practice, everything always worked out. There was a time I was short on my account and I got so upset for a second, and then I took a breather, surrendered, and trusted everything would work out. And guess what? I got an unexpected check in my account. Some will say this is luck but it's not. It's because I TRULY believe that no matter what, everything always works out, and God has my back.

I am sharing everything with you from experience. As I mentioned above, I see myself when I am in the lack, frustration, scarcity mindset, and how things are forced and don't work out. I just end up burning myself out. BUT when I practice these tools and strategies and do the work, I am more in flow. As I mentioned, life happens and we are human. Things may not go our way, and we begin to feel overwhelmed. When that happens and I do the work, as mentioned, I get different results and everything works out. The key is not to stress and be fearful. The key is to trust and believe. Ask yourself right now, how much do you truly believe in yourself? And trust me, some days you will feel the belief and have all the confidence. Then there will be days that you feel like you are ready to throw in the towel and quit your business, but having these tools and strategies will help you.

Before we dive into the tips I want to talk to you about the "Fear of Success" and the "Fear of Failure."

Both these fears have major impacts because they will affect how you show up in everyday life.

When it comes to fear, more people have that fear of success rather than failure and this can be because of more responsibilities, fear of changes in relationships, and so on. So what happens? Subconsciously, people self-sabotage themselves, not taking the full action they need to.

Here is one last thing I want to talk about before giving you the tips. Money is not evil, money is not a bad thing, and money does not make you greedy. Society can teach us or the people around us that having more money changes the person to turn them into something they are not. That is not the money, that is the person. MONEY IS NEEDED TO LIVE THE LIFE YOU ARE DESTINED TO AND HELP CHANGE THE WORLD FOR THE BETTER! YOU NEED MONEY.

Happiness starts from within, but with money, you can do more of those things without worry and stress, always thinking about how you are going to pay the next bills.

See, my friend, I am sharing all of this gold with you because I know you want to build your empire, be successful, and have the time and financial freedom so you can be with your kids, doing all the things you love and not worrying if you are going to miss your kids' sports games or how you are going to pay the rent. Trust me, I am not where I want to be right now in my business and financially, but I am well on my way there because these tools have helped me so much. I am stronger and more confident. I trust and know everything works out, and I love money.

Another thing is don't let the noise of people hold you back. If you don't have the result you desire fully, but have the strategy on how to achieve it, you are on your way, and two steps ahead of the game. It doesn't mean people shouldn't work with you. You have your passion, your talents, your knowledge, and your expertise. YOUR OWN STORY. You don't have to have thousands of clients signed on daily, living in a mansion, just to be that coach for people to work with you, showing the proof you are doing it. What do you think those other coaches like? Even Tony Robbins or Marie Forleo started from somewhere too. You have what it takes. Your experience is yours, and you have the unique touch of how you will reach and help your clients. The most important thing is you know how you will do it, you have your experience, your triumph you overcame and that is what you take to create and solve the problem for your clients giving them the result they desire with your coaching program.

Having these tools will help you with your mindset and MONEY. So let's dive in and start talking about this.

AWARENESS

I always say this: in order for you to change, you need to become aware of your thoughts, beliefs, and actions. We covered this in the beginning but take some time and question your beliefs and thoughts about money. Look at those times you signed all those clients and then those times when things weren't working out. What were you doing differently? How were you feeling?

What are your childhood memories about money? What were you taught and told about money?

God doesn't want us to be poor. We need money to make an impact in the world and do great things in life.

One thing I recently learned about myself is that I was self-sabotaging myself because I was fearful that if I was rich I would have to help EVERYONE or else I would be greedy, and no, I don't need to help everyone, and neither do you. You get to choose where your money goes, how you spend it, and how you help the world. No one tells you anything because you are the one making the money; it's your life.

I want to share when we talk about money. Start becoming aware of how you talk about money in front of your kids. Do you talk to them about money in a scarcity mindset or more of an abundance mindset?

Where are you in your business right now? Are you making money? Are you stuck on a plateau? Are you not making anything? You have to become aware of your thoughts and actions. Do not blame the economy, or that it's hard to sign on clients, or say that you tried this and nothing is working. IT'S YOUR MINDSET!

REWIRING YOUR MONEY MINDSET

Once you become aware of everything, it's time to do the rewiring. Now, there are many ways you can do this, but I like the old-fashioned ways of using affirmations. You can listen to them at night and even first thing in the morning. Another thing I like to do is write all my limiting beliefs out and replace them with the truth. Also, when things go my way, I like to celebrate, but also when the limiting fears arise, I look for proof when things worked out in the past to assure me. Let's face it, our brain likes to play tricks on us. You can teach this to your kids too. You can also find an affirmation that you like and that resonates with you and repeat it over and over. Have it as an alert pop-up on your phone three times daily and write it out on a note. See the thing with affirmations is you HAVE to believe. YOU HAVE TO FULLY BELIEVE.

FORGIVE PAST MISTAKES

Forgiveness is a big part of your healing journey. There is so much research behind this. Learn how to forgive yourself for past mistakes including how you handled money. Be gentle with yourself. Don't hold those grudges. You have to release all that no longer serves you, and this includes any mistakes you are holding onto. A lot of times, we can carry that mom guilt, so look at what you need to let go of and what you will let go of right now. We tend to be our worst critic, so it's time to be more gentle with ourselves. Know that no one is perfect. Holding on to any regret and shame can be so much more damaging, even for your own health, and we all know that your health is your true wealth.

GRATITUDE

The key to achieving all that you want is being happy and present in the moment NOW. What are you grateful for right now that you have? Try this exercise every night before bed. Journal 30 things you are grateful for that happened today. Whether small or big, list them all out, and include all the good things that have happened that day. When you write all this down, you get into the state where your vibration is up. You're feeling good, and like attracts like. What you focus on, you create more of in your life. So, if you focus on all the good that is happening, signing on clients, having fun with your kids, etc, guess what your brain will look for more of? For example, if you are focusing on why it's hard to sign on clients and you are overwhelmed all the time, your brain is going to point out all the things and SHOW YOU PROOF. You will attract all these things you don't want. So, gratitude is so big, and by practicing it daily, you can be on your way. Even for the money you receive, whether it is $3.00 you win in a lottery or double that, be excited and say, "Thank you!" " I am so grateful and happy that money just comes to me so easily and effortlessly in expected and unexpected ways."

GET SUPPORT & READ MONEY MINDSET BOOKS

Doing the money mindset work can get tricky, and it's best to really dive deep and educate yourself or even hire a coach. There are many great books you can read. You do not have to do this journey alone and trust me, you don't want to run a business alone. Why is it taking you longer than expected? When you have guidance, you can do it quicker.

Mind you, you will be taking action daily but you have the road map to success.

KNOW WHERE YOUR MONEY IS GOING

This is a big one. You have to respect money. When I didn't track my money, I was all over the place. And it is true - if you want more money, you can have more if you are showing that you respect money. When I worked with a money mindset coach, she taught me such amazing things that I use every day. One thing was having weekly money dates. Now this is a game changer because I always did monthly money planning, and I would be all over the place. It took too much time, and I dreaded looking at how much I was going to have to spend and thinking about how I was going to make things work. Now, every Thursday (I use Thursdays to plan out my business and personal schedules, my money planning, and also my cleaning, etc.), I make tea, light a candle, put music on, and even at times I'll meditate or do some breathwork. I make it fun, and I work on my budgeting. When I am on track with my money, everything runs smoothly and everything is up to date. Even at times when I did my budgeting and was wondering how I would make it work, I learned to surrender and practiced these tools. Everything always worked out.

BREATHWORK, MEDITATION, AFFIRMATIONS, VISUALIZATION, JOURNALING

These are so powerful and needed on your mompreneurial journey. I add these to my morning and night routine. Of course, I switch it up, but this will help and transform your mindset and life. They help you regulate your nervous system, help you be more present and intentional, more productive, and reprogram your subconscious mind. It's your one-stop to doing the inner and mindset work. The result is jumping into your higher version, next self. You feel vibrant and high-energy like you are tackling all your goals. Something so powerful with these is that you have the opportunity to really step into your higher version of self as I mentioned. The key is to be her now. Visualize and journal about your ideal day and how much money you make. Write out a statement and read it daily. Write out what you are doing and the actions you are taking and step into that and start being her now, doing those things now. It will bring you to your success faster with the key of feeling it as you already have it being happy now. FEEL RICH. Buy yourself a nice wallet and put money in there.

Take these tips and implement them into your daily life. Get support and start reading money mindset books. This is key in running your business because if you have money wounds that are affecting your self-worth and belief in yourself, it is going to be a long journey. Just like mine. I made things much more difficult for myself than they already were. I am far more along than where I used to be but I wish I knew this before and that it didn't take me so long. BUT I acknowledge where I am because I know I am where I need to be. I know where I am headed, and the right direction is smoother. So there's no perfect way but you have to believe and trust in yourself. Remember, when times get tough, surrender to God. He, or whoever you believe in, is here to help because, at the end of the day, there is a Higher Power. It isn't just you. It's time to stop running the show on your own, let go of the wheel, and let your Higher Power in to help you. BUT that means you have to do the work too. This will help transform your life and business, but most importantly, it will change how you show up being a mom. Being present and intentional. When you work through any of your limiting beliefs, you become an unstoppable force because, at the end of the day, that is what is holding you back. So say it with me with belief: "I love money and money loves me. Money comes to me easily and effortlessly. Money comes to me in expected and unexpected ways."

If you would like to connect, have a free, 15-minute strategy call and talk about where you are feeling held back in your business. We can find a strategy that can help you move forward so you can start showing up more confidently and reaching your next level of success. Feel free to send me an email at ashleythemompreneurcoach@gmail.com

I also created a 1:1 Elevate 3 Month Coaching Program where we dive deep, do the inner work, and expand your mindset so you can confidently show up and reach your next level of success. Also, I have a 4 Week Sprint Program "More Abundance," and this is a program where we will dive into releasing those limiting beliefs and creating a strategy you walk away with that you can use to level up in your business and life.

I hope you take away all the gold nuggets here in this chapter and this whole book. These are stories you can relate to but also tools and strategies that you can start implementing into your everyday life. Mompreneurship doesn't have to be a lonely, frustrating ride; it can be fun, and it's a blast when you have your community of women supporting and cheering you on daily. Use these tools to make your life simpler. You will see the ripple effect it has on guiding you to be a more confident entrepreneur, showing up for yourself and your clients but also most importantly for your kiddos. In order to grow, you have to nurture yourself. One thing I have learned is that when you turn to God and you take your hands off the wheel, everything else runs more smoothly. Always remember that fear and belief don't go together. The fear will come at times but you can shake it off. You use these tools and others like going to the gym, nature, walks, and having more fun. Everything will always work out. I know when I get overwhelmed, I plant the seeds. I do the work, and then I take my hands off the wheel. I let go and let God in, and let me tell you, with the belief and trust I have, EVERYTHING ALWAYS DOES WORK OUT. AND IF IT DOESN'T, THERE IS SOMETHING BETTER AND GREATER AHEAD.

Be excited and know where you are going. You have talents that no one else has. You are your own unique self, so no one is going to come save you. You are not broken BUT YOU HAVE TO BELIEVE IN YOURSELF. Take action daily, focus on your non-negotiables, and make sure to do them daily. Trust me, it will all work out and come to a place. The only way it won't work out is when you stop and quit. So, everything comes down to the choices you make and how you are going to be intentional with all your actions. Are you going to knowingly just sit on the couch and scroll through your phone, or are you going to knowingly and intentionally take the action you planned out? When you do all this and fully step in your power, sharing daily about the results you give, being visible, and being authentic, you will attract your dream life and dream clients to you easily and effortlessly. It's about strategizing but most importantly it's doing the inner and mindset work, Queen.

Amber Till

Founder & CEO of The ART Skool

https://www.facebook.com/groups/womenserenityseekers
linktr.ee/atill22

Amber Renee Till is a much sought after expert in equipping anxious mompreneurs with an evidence-based technique, so they can build a successful business without sacrificing their family. Achieving bestseller status in 2023 landed her on national platforms like NBC, and in March 2024, Amber's resilience narrative became worldwide as the cover feature of BAUW.

She founded The ART Skool in 2023, which was created by merging her initials, her love for art, and focusing on her three-step transformative ART Metamorphosis Process. Amber is a beacon of hope in the realm of mental health, defying societal silence, and delving into inherited patterns.

Amber embodies self-care and passion pursuit, showcasing her journey from obscurity to multifaceted success while prioritizing family. Through her personal challenges, triumphs, and global initiatives, Amber empowers women to break free from the chains of crippling anxiety. To learn more about Amber, visit www.linktr.ee/atill22.

BREAKING CHAINS: FROM ANXIETY TO METAMORPHOSIS MASTERY - MY JOURNEY OF FINDING CLARITY AS A MOMPRENEUR

By Amber Till

My heart literally sank to my stomach as I watched our one-and-a-half-year-old son tumble down the flight of stairs as I stood in the kitchen, attached to my phone and computer.

The moment he hit the floor, during that life-changing moment for me, absolutely nothing else mattered besides him.

Luckily, there wasn't even a bruise on him, but that moment will forever be stitched into my brain.

Our son was a little behind on his gross motor skills and he was just starting to learn about the stairs.

I was so focused on my work and trying to achieve my goals that I did not even realize he had gotten around the baby gate and started crawling up the stairs. He made it about six or seven steps before I saw him tumbling backward, head first.

My husband came running with terror as he heard the loud thud of our son hitting the floor.

I will never forget the look on my husband's face.

Our frightened son only cried for about one minute.

My tears lasted a lot longer.

I had no words. I knew I had really messed up. My guilt over that situation haunted me for quite a while.

All I ever wanted to be since I was young was a mother. I could not wait to love my babies just as my mom had always loved me. That unconditional love and protection she and my stepdad showed me was unmatched.

Yet, I did not protect my son at that moment.

It was April 2022 and I was wrapping up my first year in an MLM business that I had joined to help empower women. The company and leadership ranks had me consumed with "winning." I was doing amazing, moving up quickly, achieving goals, earning diamond rings, earning trips, etc.

Everyone was so proud of me.

But it was all external. I knew deep down that external things would never bring anyone value or true happiness.

I was not winning, nor did I feel proud of myself at all. A huge realization came over me that my business kept me from one of the most important things in my life.

Everyone who was so proud and inspired by me did not see this accident. They did not even care much when I tried to share about it either.

I was traumatized by how much I messed up. I let my son down more in that moment than I will ever do again in my lifetime.

Working online was such a huge blessing for me for many reasons, but I never thought I would let my mind get so consumed by it.

I have multiple health conditions, and I love staying home with my children to raise them, so the online space is perfect for me. But at what cost? Luckily, I now have found the solution.

I started my online entrepreneurial journey in a different MLM business in October 2020.

We all know what happened in March 2020, but I also gave birth to our son in June 2020. I felt very lonely even though my parents and husband were amazing throughout all of it.

I was scared for my family living in the new unknown certainties of everything. I missed connecting with people outside, so I looked for more online.

Learning the ends and outs of running a business, and also re-learning Facebook after being off it for ten years, was a lot to take on at first. However, I enjoyed bringing in a little extra money for my family since my husband is the sole provider.

The MLM company and people were amazing. I grew a large team and loved all of the new connections.

Soon after realizing that business was not going to bring in consistent income, I decided to join a second MLM business. I felt like I should have been making more money for as much effort as I was pouring into the first business.

As I mentioned, I did well managing the two businesses and really succeeding with the business goals.

I loved helping people with different needs and spoiling them with free stuff every so often. Between free shipping and little gifts, it added a whole new level to the personalized care I could give.

The connections I made because of these two businesses kept me in them longer than I should have stayed, looking back.

When my customers became my friends, I never wanted to let them down.

I just now realized those companies weren't good for me because I wanted so much more out of them than what was ultimately available.

It was no secret that I had both businesses, alongside taking care of two small children, plus running our household as a wife and stay-at-home mom.

Before having children, I was a nanny for ten years, and I absolutely loved that role of helping different families.

After having our daughter, our firstborn almost eight years ago now, life quickly changed, and I didn't help as many other families as before. Then with the pandemic and the birth of our son, I was missing that caregiving part of me.

I have always wanted to help people and these opportunities gave me that chance. Both companies were wonderful stepping stones for me. I learned a lot from each one.

The stress and the pressure started adding up, though. My husband would notice me being more upset with him and the kids. I would "snap" and yell more often than I care to admit. I would cry and be so disappointed if I did not hit a business goal in time. Then, I would cry more because I wasn't being the best wife and mother to them.

The guilt and sadness of being unbalanced was horrible.

The pressure put on today's modern woman is unrelenting. She must excel in her career, be a great homemaker, perfect wife, amazing mother, wonderful cook, involved in her community, and do it all while looking in shape and "put together."

That is not pressure from most spouses; that is pressure from the outside world. It is no wonder women are stressed out and exhausted.

If one of our kids were sick and it kept me away from my work, I would be so upset with the situation.

I was literally addicted to my businesses and succeeding in them.

The myth most women buy into, including me, is that we must be superheroes. In return, this leaves us all feeling inadequate, unhappy, anxious, and depressed.

I lost sight of why I even joined these businesses in the first place. My main goal was to have fun, make friends, earn a little extra money, and enjoy my family and friends more. It quickly became quite the opposite.

God was really looking over our son that day because he could have been seriously injured. And when the business that I was trying so hard to grow didn't even really care what had happened, I knew God was telling me something much bigger.

I got so caught up in the wrong dream. I lost sight of who I was.

Never in my life did I ever care about earning jewelry. Material things have never brought me happiness. And for a split second, I forgot that and changed my beliefs.

I started to dim my light for the sake of the whole.

However, my eyes were finally opened back up.

A huge dark cloud of envy, lust, ego, worry, and stress slowly began releasing from around me. I had been suffocating under the pressure of society's "norms."

This was not the first time in my life that I noticed the patterns of what I was doing, but I am confident it will be the last.

Generation after generation we are told how to look, dress, speak, plus so much more. We do not talk about things such as miscarriage, abuse, alcoholism, your child being addicted to drugs, your spouse cheating, money, divorce, businesses falling apart, assault…none of it.

"What will people think?!"

It is frowned upon if it's anything that's less than "ideal" or "perfect."

My son falling down the stairs did not matter because that was not the image I was "supposed" to be portraying.

I wish I had told more people about the pressure it caused me to lose sight of my son at that moment.

It quickly became very apparent who was actually in my corner, rooting for me for the right reasons.

For many of us, our generational curse is anger, no communication, and a lot of avoidance. We come from a long line of people who act like nothing happened. They think they can "hide" it all away, which is unhealthy and doesn't work.

Those negative habits are then programmed into us.

Another thing we learned is that we should not indulge the ego with self-affirmations, so when we do try to love ourselves, it feels like a sin. It must all be re-trained in our brains far below the surface.

The pressure from society and the generational patterns of never talking about our emotions has led to the biggest problem most people aren't even aware of having because it is so ingrained into our minds.

If only I knew then what I know now.

My husband was lost, watching me spiral out of control. I was turning into something he could only try to get me to realize I was becoming long before I realized it myself.

But I needed that moment from God.

I hate that our son was the victim, but my love for him awoke me.

It was me that needed to change, not the world around me.

Trying to change the world around me was ever-evolving, and I thought that external change would help eliminate my stress and overwhelm.

I would try everything but no matter what new shiny object came around or quick fix, nothing got better.

Usually, it got worse.

Constant limiting beliefs that I had programmed into myself out of habit such as, "I can't handle this pressure," "I am a failure," or "I can't do this anymore, something has to change," had me stuck in a cycle of anxiety that took over every experience I took part in.

I needed to face my fears head-on, the real issues that lay underneath the surface, and figure out what really made me have huge insecurities about who I was.

If that wasn't a big enough sign for God, a couple of months after our son's accidental fall, a close family member found out they had lung cancer. This is news no one ever wants to hear. But family was officially my top priority.

My businesses took a very far back seat, and I was ok with that. The anxiety was no longer consuming me, and my head was clear on what I wanted, and that was family.

The surgery went well, thankfully, that September, and life has adjusted some since then for us all. I could not imagine being anywhere else other than with my family during that time.

I am so thankful to those who were truly there for me that year and beyond.

I am thankful for my husband and his career to always be our crutch, but at the same time, I have always dreamed of being able to help our family more financially.

Without people believing in me, I would not be who I am today. That is why finding a great mentor you align with is so important for your future. Everyone has a mentor, but you must find someone with a lot of the same values.

Your values truly are most important.

I also started missing my passion for helping others since I had taken a huge step back months before. I started feeling hopeless again but knew deep down that there was more for me out there.

I started journaling more, playing games or doing puzzles, and reflecting on what really mattered most to me.

So many business ideas swarmed my brain every day as I searched for what God was calling me to do.

In late 2022, I joined my very first online training. I initially thought it would help me with the MLM businesses I was in, but I gained so much more than I could have ever believed I would.

The perspective it gave me and the personal development pieces of it were very transformative.

My mind shifted from working harder to working smarter with my businesses, and I wanted to pass it along to my "sisters" in the companies. I felt like I hit the breakthrough I was searching for.

I wanted to help them grow their teams and be successful without taking anything from them in return.

We were all a team in my mind.

My ultimate goal was to help them not be consumed by the fears and stress of the business as I had previously felt.

I thought I could help them determine what was important, schedule their time better, breathe throughout the day to clear their mind, have better self-esteem, and show them that it is possible to be happy and successful.

Step by step, I started guiding them and teaching them.

But, unfortunately, the excitement I had found through helping them quickly became the feeling of disappointment again as my upline told me to stop helping the other women in the company. She did not want them to come to me for answers.

Confused by her reaction, I stopped doing it out of respect.

So, I went back to the training to start following and learning from the lady who taught the classes. Her business of helping so many people no matter what they were doing really connected well with me.

Those who judged that woman were also the ones who did not understand why I was so upset that my son rolled down the stairs since he ended up being completely fine, not worrying about how I felt.

All red flags, right?

Little steps forward in a new direction each and every day became my new normal. I prayed every day and knew that I could not do this journey alone.

At this point, I had gone almost 30 years feeling silenced for the abuse I experienced as a young child, and that kept me in an internal place of disarray. It was hard to have high self-esteem and think that I was ever worthy of success.

Tears were never far behind when I used to handle most situations.

Anything and everything would make me cry because I was in constant fight or flight mode. That inner fear of not knowing what to do or what to say when trying to express myself was always there.

I never learned a healthy emotional resilience pattern before.

So many people are labeled as "mental health patients" since they have anxiety and depression, and I am here to stop the stigma around this.

It may be true that they feel those things, but in fact, they just feel more than most.

They/we have a gift of feeling.

We all know you can't heal the pain you refuse to feel. Pain demands to be felt, which is why I started on this path from God to help others.

I have been through more in this lifetime than most, and those negative thought patterns I had for the majority of my life kept me feeling not good enough when I wasn't "perfect" or "succeeding."

We become loyal and comfortable in our fear and the relentless stream of self-criticism.

It was incredibly hard to change a habit I have had that long (decades), but I knew it was possible. I needed to love myself more and be proud of myself for everything I had gone through.

I am proud of myself for realizing then that I deserved better for myself and my family.

Not even one year after my son's accidental fall, February 2023 marked ten years of my big brother's angel anniversary. From the months leading up to this anniversary, plus the significance of an entire decade of him being taken from us, a fire was lit under me.

There was no more guessing and searching. I knew God's plan for me was big, and I was ready to listen and receive.

February 27, 2013, was such a tragic day for my family and me. I talk about it more in another book I was a part of, but ultimately, my brother was shot and killed over drugs. My heart still weeps for him and the life he could have had. He was an amazing brother, son, friend, etc.

Losing him to drugs and alcohol a couple of years before he was killed was a very difficult time to navigate. I was not in the best mental state either, but I never turned to those negative coping outlets personally.

As both victims of childhood abuse, we were constantly told not to talk about it. Everyone who knew what happened would just tell us they were sorry or how awful the person who abused us truly was.

I wish people would have made me feel less like an "outcast" and more accepted that it wasn't anything to be ashamed of so my bottled-up feelings wouldn't have led to so much anxiety.

Trust, love for others and myself, and not feeling alone were taken from me at a very young age.

It is honestly frustrating to look back and remember feeling so much shame and guilt for something someone else did to me. I did not do anything wrong. It took me years of therapy to finally release that. It should be the abuser feeling shame and guilt.

It also took me years of therapy to let go of the guilt I felt that I survived and my brother didn't. My family and I tried to get my brother help and become sober, but it was too big of a battle for us. He chose to escape his thoughts and feelings in one of the worst ways possible and paid the ultimate price.

Shortly after the decade anniversary of his death, I was randomly asked to be a part of another collaboration book from the publisher. I was very hesitant but had always thought about writing my story and figured starting with one chapter would be the perfect healing process I needed to talk about why mental health is so important to me.

That journey of writing last year was everything I thought it would be. I laughed and cried tears of sadness and happiness, but ultimately, I was so proud of myself for doing it. I knew God sent me that opportunity for a reason.

Because of that opportunity and the need to promote my business at the end of the chapter, it became very apparent that I needed to think about what exact business I was going to be promoting.

So, in June 2023, my LLC business was officially in the books. The ART Skool was established, and it still makes me smile to this day to think about all of my dreams coming true.

I merged my initials (Amber Renee Till) with my love for art. I also created my easy three-step transformative ART Metamorphosis Process that I use to help other mompreneurs find clarity and balance between running their successful business without sacrificing their family. I am teaching that exact system for free in my latest masterclass. Where upon joining, you will receive multiple free bonuses to help in your business. I am also excitedly introducing my brand-new cohort, Metamorphosis Mastery Circle.

By being a certified Rapid Reprogramming Coach, I am able to teach the women within my Cohort how to implement Rapid Reprogramming into their own lives within just twelve short weeks. This powerful brain training method helps liberate women from worry at its root and is going to help empower so many around the world. I offer a lot more powerful tools via my Metamorphosis Mastery Circle, but you'll have to catch my masterclass to learn more!

Seeing how I know from my past what it feels like to be "lost" and alone, constantly uncertain by my racing thoughts, I never want anyone else to feel like that. So, one of the very first things I did upon starting my own business was create a free Facebook group, Women Serenity Seekers.

I am extremely proud of the safe, exclusive, non-triggering, non-judgmental private group I created. I call the ladies in there my "metamorphosisters" for fun. These ladies inspire me every day by being there and acknowledging that they want a better life for themselves. They are all taking an amazing first step towards freedom from anxiety.

Being a beacon of hope in the realm of mental health and defying societal silence is no small order to achieve. But as a Metamorphosis

Mentor, I aid women battling anxiety, delving into inherited patterns that most do not even realize we acquired at early ages.

I have learned how to balance multiple roles and embody self-care and passion pursuit, all while showcasing my journey from obscurity to multifaceted success and still prioritizing my family.

I truly love working with women seeking solutions beyond harmful coping mechanisms (i.e. alcohol, drugs, prescriptions, etc) and who have tried other techniques but still feel anxiety keeps them from living their best life.

After decades of talk therapy, trying EMDR and not accepting it well, plus so many other techniques, Rapid Reprogramming was/is the ultimate game-changer for me. In just a few short months after learning my mentor's signature method, I had the ultimate breakthrough.

I trained and studied for hours with her help guiding me to become certified in RR myself where I am now able to teach it to others.

It is not unsafe, hypnosis, or plain positive talk. I am teaching you how to release the worry in your brain from the source.

I learned to explain it as instead of taking Tylenol for your headache, we work together to remove the source of the headache, so Tylenol is not needed.

I cannot tell you what a relieving feeling it was to let go of 30+ years of fear and worry.

Besides my own huge breakthrough, the women I have worked with one-on-one had amazing sessions with me where we would both leave in happy tears. Their relief brought tears to their eyes as well as made me so happy for them and proud I could help.

Many of the women I work with have had different fears about starting or running their own businesses. But in all cases, their anxiety was keeping them stuck and afraid to go after their dreams. I definitely started seeing a pattern and ways I could help them because I also had those fears of starting my own business myself.

One of the women I worked with, Anne, worried about going on a month-long trip to see family and wasn't sure how she would keep up her business while being away. But I helped guide her, in just one session alone, which helped re-train her brain to show her proof that it would be possible.

Another woman I worked with, Beth, struggled to start her business because she did not want to show her face online due to past trauma. It was amazing to help her break through these negative thoughts that were holding her back.

Charlotte worried about moving to a different country and starting her business there. The fear of feeling like she was starting over, knowing no one in a brand new country, kept her stuck. I truly loved sparking her interest and excitement again as we made some big changes to her negative, deep-rooted beliefs.

Kandice worried about starting her own business because she simply felt inadequate. Years of telling herself she wasn't good enough was not helping her move forward. This was powerful for me to help guide her since I connected so well to those thoughts.

And my last testimonial comes from Lisa, who I connected with for deeper reasons. She was worried about starting her business and not having enough time for her family. The anxiety and guilt consumed her. Sitting with her (across screens on Zoom) as she truly felt the beliefs changed, we both had tears flowing. It was such a powerful metamorphosis that day.

Feeling uncertain and stuck for most of my life, I did not feel the path forward because I was so held down by the chains from my past. I had the desire but never felt the way out, just like these women.

"My family and I deserve better," I constantly told myself. Our children are only little once, and I see how fast time is going by for us. I used to want so badly to play with my kids instead of laying in my bed as my pillow was covered with tears.

My worries and fears would paralyze me.

Besides crying, my stomach was always upset, especially under stress with a racing heart, so much fatigue, and multiple headaches a week.

My thoughts would go to the worst-case scenario, hyper-focusing, or black-and-white thinking. Nothing was positive, and I was always in freak-out mode.

Besides my relationships suffering, so did my sleep and my daily schedule since I was all over the place. The slightest little thing that was out of order would throw me into a tizzy.

Nothing got done after "working" for several hours because of the racing thoughts and unorganized thinking.

I wanted to literally hide away in my bed from the world because it was all just too overwhelming.

Then, I felt guilty for missing out.

Now, I am able to enjoy being around others and be more present in the moment. The messy living room and the dirty dishes can wait. I know I will find time to make things happen because I am able to see more clarity every day now.

I started having more positive and calm inner dialogues, telling myself things such as, "I can handle this one step at a time," or "I am good enough just as I am."

I wasted a lot of my life worrying about how things would happen, but not anymore, and that in itself is life-changing.

The more inner peace I cultivated, the less external circumstances would start to bother me. I realized how much power I have in choosing my attitude and gratitude regardless of what is happening around me.

My mission is to help women, and that, as a ripple effect, helps the world. I want you to become your best version of yourself, living more fulfilling and anxiety-free without caving into unrealistic, external expectations.

Momma, no more hiding the pain with negative outlets after we work together.

Stop the generational patterns, and learn how to safely break the chains of negative thought habits creating your pain.

You will begin to feel worthy, have more patience and understanding with others, less sadness and resentment, less insecurities, less guilt, and most importantly, less overwhelming thoughts that cause most of the pain.

When you stop trying to control the universe, the universe opens up more opportunities and better relationships and ultimately flows better altogether.

You will no longer feel desperate to seek joy; you will find it from within.

Choose affection over perfection. We deserve grace, self-love, and self-care without all of the pressure of being "perfect."

It is never too late to learn how to have an emotionally resilient inner voice, and it is much better to pass it on. To learn more about Amber, search Facebook for the Women Serenity Seekers group and visit www.linktr.ee/atill22.

Christina Whiteley

Life Transformed
Business Freedom Leader

https://www.linkedin.com/in/christinawhiteley
https://www.facebook.com/christina.whiteley.54
https://www.instagram.com/thechristinawhiteley
https://christina-whiteley.mykajabi.com/christina-whiteley-go-to-links

Christina, a natural-born entrepreneur and advocate for purpose-driven business, continually evolves her ventures to reflect her values. As a freedom-driven mother, she aims to empower others to succeed while prioritizing family time. After years of owning a salon and wedding business, Christina sought deeper impact. Her journey into business strategy, online marketing, and leadership began with the birth of her daughter. Now, Christina guides individuals on seeking freedom through creative business strategies.

Through podcasts, speaking engagements, and social media, she shares insights for crafting multiple income streams and pursuing passions outside traditional constraints. Under her brand, Life Transformed, Christina leads "The 6 Figure Profit Plan" Mastermind program, assisting entrepreneurs to break through income barriers strategically. Her mission is to inspire purpose-centered businesses, offering entrepreneurs the tools to create fulfilling lives while achieving financial success without burnout.

ENTREPRENEURIAL FREEDOM; THE GREATEST GIFT YOU CAN GIVE YOUR CHILDREN

By Christina Whiteley

As I sit down to write and share my journey of mompreneurship with you, the irony is not lost on me that I am exhausted, sleep-deprived, and operating on empty as I gave birth to my second child six weeks ago. I'm also living my dream life by the beach in Cabo San Lucas, Mexico doing what I love every single day. I'm the CEO of my company, Life Transformed, where I teach entrepreneurs how to find business freedom by creating an income around the lifestyle they desire. Because I believe that if you don't, you'll end up missing out on the things that matter most to you. I also launched a new business nine weeks ago (yes, three weeks before my baby was born), because I can't say no to a great opportunity that is aligned with my values and mission.

I believe in being an example, and this year I am determined to create yet another six-figure income within six months to show moms like you that it is possible to create a significant amount of money while being a present and conscious parent. However, it doesn't mean that it is perfectly executed. I wish someone had saved me all the time I spent in my head thinking about HOW to execute what I wanted. So I'll do you a favor and share the secret right up front: we do it messy. We use imperfect action to find our way forward and fine-tune the details in real-time by using feedback from our customers or clients. We simply commit to figuring it out. Then, we master it and continue to grow, pushing through the barriers we faced before.

I remember saying to my mentor one time, "THIS IS SO HARD," when I had to learn some new skills that challenged me and leveled up my mindset. The inner work, the adversity you need to overcome, and the level of growth required to get to the top... "How can I do this AND be a mom?" She said, "Never forget you GET to build this life. You GET to build it with joy, and there are no rules. If you think this is hard, what do you think of the alternative?" She got me there.

This life is not for the faint of heart, but it is for sure the most rewarding, as I have the most incredible ideation sessions with my firstborn, who is now eight, on what kind of business she wants to create and who she wants to help "when she grows up." Not a lot of kids have experienced what she has at her age; living in another country, learning another language, travelling around the world, and meeting new people while experiencing different cultures. I truly believe travel is one of the best ways to get an education, so we have made it a priority.

When I was a child and people asked me what I wanted to be when I grew up, I didn't say a doctor, a teacher, or even a veterinarian... I told people that I couldn't wait to be a mom. I knew my calling was to raise kind and thoughtful kids who would truly make a difference in the world. The desire to coach others came much later in life when I realized I could monetize my serial entrepreneurial experiences, 20+ years of personal development, as well as the dozens of skillsets I'd learned in online sales, marketing, and branding over the last eight years. I knew I could help other moms create a life where they could have kids and build financial stability too. Plus, I NEVER wanted to ever have to ask for permission to spend money, or God forbid, someone used the word "budget" in front of me because I would for sure break out in hives. I wanted to make enough money so that I could have a family, travel the world with them, and never have to worry about checking my bank account or having maxed-out credit cards. I knew what I wanted, but I didn't know how to create it. However, it was something I was excited to get out of bed every morning to pursue. Having a goal big enough to set your soul on fire is the one thing that will keep you motivated even when things are hard and you feel like giving up.

I knew very early on that having a boss was not for me. I loved working for myself, making my own rules, and never being stifled by those who saw my ambition as a threat. I wanted to show other women that you can become a self-made millionaire and that there are multiple roads that lead to that destination that do not exclude you from being at home and raising your kids.

No, this doesn't happen overnight, but it WILL happen if you create a plan and work intentionally towards what you want – creating an income that allows you to have the option to live life on your terms.

However, before I got here, I was duped by society and did what was expected of me. I was raised by two parents who had blue-collar jobs. They worked hard and we never went without; however, growing up, my idea of success was to get a good job where I could pay my bills and afford to live in a nice house. Entrepreneurship wasn't modelled for me, but it was clearly in my heart as I started my first business delivering papers I'd pick up at the corner store and sell for a dollar more, then selling candles I had made to my neighbours at the age of eight. As expected of me, I got good grades, and went to university for the only thing I truly loved, music. Then I went to school to become a hairstylist because, at 23, I realized the life of a musician wasn't conducive to having a family and being present. By doing hair, I could make my own schedule, and eventually, I started working for myself and ran a home-based salon as well as an on-site wedding business. Even though I had people working for me at this time, I wasn't able to save any money and wondered how I could cross that six-figure-a-year mark while trading time for money with the cost of doing business on the rise. It was late in my pregnancy when I had a debilitating shoulder injury that I realized I had to do something different.

Tomorrow isn't promised, so I wasn't about to wait for retirement to start living my life the way I truly wanted to. We get to decide, and every decision we make either leads us closer or farther away from our goals and how we want to live our lives, true to our aligned purpose. Whether that's raising incredible children who pave the way for the next generation, taking on a career that you feel divinely connected and called to do, or navigating entrepreneurship while traveling the world, we truly can have it all if we flow in synergy with what we've been divinely called to do.

The world has changed, and in order to get ahead you have to be willing to do more than most to have options other people don't have. I didn't want to go get a job; I wanted to raise my kids and be an example for them. I wanted them to be mentored by me first. I also wanted to make more money than a job would pay while having the freedom and flexibility in my schedule and realized that, without a business, the majority of my money would go to taxes. The system is set up to fail you, and it's important you realize this sooner rather than later and do everything in your power to increase your financial literacy so you and your family can win too. We get our money mindset ingrained in us from our parents, so having a dad who grew up on welfare and a mom who, for the majority of her life, was at home with us didn't provide the education I needed to thrive in this lifetime of change and technology.

The other thing we don't often talk about is what we have to give up in this process. People get to see the highlight reel, but they don't know what has gone on behind closed doors. I remember in my early years having to give up going out with my girlfriends on the weekend because I would have 5 am wake-up calls almost every weekend to travel to a destination to do wedding hair. I had to choose business over my social life time and time again as the years went on. My travel became centered around masterminds and business conventions or leadership retreats. I still work on the weekends, it just looks a little different now.

That's not to say that I don't take time off. I just do it when I want and have integrated what I do into my daily life because I truly love it, and it doesn't feel like work.

I also had to learn how valuable my time was, and if I wasn't being present with my family, I had to be very intentional with the people who I spent time with. I once had a friend say to me, Christina, you've been leveling up your friends and outgrowing people since I met you 15 years ago. When he said that something clicked. For many years I thought I had lost friends due to my big dreams and desire to work more than most. I continued to learn and grow, yet many stayed the same. There are very few people in this life who will stick with you and love you at every stage of your growth – love those people with everything you have because when you grow, it makes many feel uncomfortable simply because it's a reflection of them not doing the same work you are. I've always wished people well and hoped to catch up with them later down the line, but I made hard decisions to spend less time with people who didn't fuel my growth.

You may even come to a point in time when the people around you aren't challenging you or encouraging you to move forward and play bigger. There have been many times that friends and family have said to me, "You should take time off, you don't need to work this hard." What they don't understand is the drive we have as entrepreneurs; it's different from the rest, and I've created a life where I love what I do so it doesn't feel like work. It's truly part of my identity and who I am.

This is where mentorship and masterminds come into play. If you want to level up your inner circle, often you have to pay for proximity you want to learn from before you've proved yourself and earned your way in. It's a small circle at the top, but one that is filled with people who will fuel your way to the top. I pay business mentors tens of thousands of dollars a year to hold me accountable and make me do the things I don't really want to do because if I didn't, I probably would sit in comfort and not pursue my highest purpose. That doesn't serve anyone. I had to pull myself out of the rooms I was comfortable in and pull up a chair around tables that I didn't think I belonged to, just to start thinking bigger and do more. As entrepreneurs, we work at a faster pace than most, and that rhythm in which we work speeds up as we take on new levels of business and a higher income. We also learn that outsourcing to experts instead of trying to do everything ourselves is what will save us from burnout and move the needle forward faster.

Who you surround yourself with matters greatly, and if they aren't pushing you to be the best version of yourself and calling you on your bullshit, they aren't helping; they are hindering. I've been through really lonely stages in business where I've felt like I've left so many behind who were holding me back, yet I've made room in those instances for truly amazing humans who have pushed me forward despite all the challenges I have faced. These people have laughed with me and sometimes cried through these moments when I just wanted to throw in the towel and dreamed of becoming a trophy wife until I came back down from where I was spinning to get to work and re-evaluate the plan in front of me.

There were many times I wanted to quit and questioned if I was truly cut out for this work. Many times I cried and crawled into bed to reset. But what I can tell you is I never quit on a bad day, and the next day was always a new beginning. Even if I still had a mountain to climb or had to work through something that challenged me, I continued to move the needle forward, inch by inch, calling in all of my resources along the way. As a high performer, not only do you need coaches, mentors, and accountability partners, but you also need counsellors, intuitive healers, and people you trust to help you work through the tough stuff and who will hold you to your highest good. You need a team of people to succeed when you're a high performer.

To evolve in business, you must constantly reflect on what you're doing to improve and adjust course. The average person writes out their goals once a year, right around the new year, and if they're good, they may even evaluate quarterly. The next level of self-development is weekly goal setting so that you can be conscious of what you need to improve and can move through failure faster. Failure becomes a game, and not one that you pout about if you lose, but instead one you celebrate because you're learning so much faster than most. You've truly hit an expert level in life and business when you can make decisions based on facts, not feelings, and you've improved your emotional intelligence to a place where you take absolute ownership of everything and all in your life and stop blaming people and circumstances for the roadblocks you will inevitably hit along the way. Many of us can get stuck in analysis paralysis which stops momentum in its tracks. So let me help you get unstuck… If you want an extraordinary life, create a habit of doing two things before you fall asleep at night. One, give gratitude for everything you have, and two, run through the day and acknowledge where you could have done things better. My secret is often reciting this mantra, "Now that I know better, I'll do better," so I don't get sucked back into the pattern of self-loathing when I make a mistake.

As you can tell, I'm not pulling any punches because I want you to understand what it takes, and what you'll have to go through to truly live joyfully with peace in your heart, AND to be a great example for your kids. They learn communication, conflict resolution, problem solving, and emotional regulation through US! So ask yourself, "What am I modeling for them on a daily basis?"

Building business is just as important to me as raising a family, so attention needs to be spent focussing on both, or else you will drop the ball somewhere. There is a reason why most career-driven people suffer in their relationships, and it's because they sacrifice too much, believing that they have to in order to succeed and create the income they desire. It's simply not true. You can have an incredible marriage that is truly a partnership and get so much more done together if you play to your strengths and ask for help when it comes to your weaknesses. Having a supportive husband who is a teammate in life has helped us build our dreams faster than I could have done alone. It doesn't mean we agreed on everything, but we were willing to compromise and make sacrifices when necessary for the greater good of our family. I am forever grateful for his support and know I wouldn't be WHO I am today, or WHERE I am today, without his belief in me. He and his brother were raised by a single mom who was their sole provider, and I honestly have so much respect for any of you who do this on your own. Your strength is unmatched, and your children are SO lucky to have you. Your support network comes from the people around you and I pray that if you are reading this now, you find the relationship you deserve for the special human that you are.

Interestingly enough, it was almost by accident I stumbled into network marketing, which I believe is one of the best real-life business development, human psychology, and leadership programs out there. You get paid to learn and develop your skills in real-time with the marketplace. To win in this space, you have to hone your skills in communication, conflict resolution, team leadership as well as sales and marketing – which led me to build a personal brand, something I think every single human can benefit from no matter what you do or what you sell. Building a community of people with whom you provide value to, learn to trust, and who you get to choose to serve and work with is one of the greatest gifts you can do for yourself.

Now, I get the stigma that comes with network marketing, but being someone who's made seven-figures in the industry, I can tell you I care a heck of a lot less about what people think, and I now strive to help those who see the vision find their freedom too. Not everyone has a business they can build, so finding a product you align with and a business in a box is one of the fastest ways I've ever seen people create wealth with very little capital. It makes financial freedom possible for anyone no matter their age, race, education level, or location. I am also a huge advocate for multiple streams of income which has served me well as we face the hardships of this moment in time with where we are in the debt cycle. Leaning into different areas of income when they make sense and serving people where they are is part of the constant reinvention of being an entrepreneur. It's constant growth, evolution, and problem-solving, although not without major challenges. You will make ten thousand dollar mistakes on your way to six-figures, and a hundred thousand dollars worth of mistakes on your way to a million... I can only assume as we continue to grow and learn that we will make a million dollars worth of mistakes on the road to consistent and multiple seven and eight-figure incomes, but that's part of the journey. I only share this with you so you come to expect it and it doesn't take you out of the game when you're going through it. We tend to beat ourselves up far too long for mistakes we've made instead of acknowledging the mistake, learning from it, and vowing to never make it again so we can move forward faster. Once it's done, it's done, and there's no point in crying over spilled milk. Most people never get what they want because they are too scared of what they could lose, and are not focussed enough on what they need to do to WIN.

Another huge life lesson has been to stop making decisions based on what you've experienced in the past, or what you are currently experiencing in life right now, and instead start making daily decisions that will get you what you want in the future. For example, if you want to spend time with your family, don't pick a career that has you working 80 hours a week where you have to work evenings and weekends. You win by using your mind and creating solutions for people who need help getting to where you are. You are in full control of the life you get to live, and although entrepreneurship is a more difficult path, it's one that is incredibly rewarding once you are able to create time and financial freedom.

The other key factor to creating success as a mompreneur is to not compare your journey to anyone else's because you are building YOUR dream. Your dream doesn't look like my dream, and it doesn't look like your sisters' or your cousins' either, and it's probably not the dream your parents had for you. If you are debt-free, work 15 hours a week, and make less than $100k a year but have everything you want, that's all that matters. As long as you are living within your means and planning for the future. We get so caught up in comparison that we often forget why we started in the first place.

We also have to honor the chapters of life we are in. You can't be full-board, all in, with a newborn or young children. I'm being reminded of that right now as I've had to stop countless times to breastfeed, rock, nurture, and play while writing this chapter. Previously, it's taken me a few hours to write a chapter, and I'm going on day five of all-day, semi-focus. I also reduced the hours I work and work very intentionally with my high-ticket clients and my new business to create residual income while we enter this phase of our life knowing how unpredictable it is. This isn't to say that I can't accomplish what I want to; I just need to spend a lot more time and focus on being present, intentional, and with gratitude as a mom in the stage we are in now. We waited almost six years with multiple miscarriages for our son to arrive, and I will not wish this time away so that I can focus on business. I embrace every stage and every moment and do the best I can daily, even if I feel like I'm not moving as quickly as I want. I've also really learned how to ask for help. You have a partner or friends and family in your circle, and if you learn how to communicate your feelings instead of getting to your breaking point and having a total meltdown, you will be able to move through these difficult times.

Speaking of difficult times... COVID changed things dramatically for us. We "woke up" so to speak and realized that even though we had this beautiful home on a 10-acre hobby farm in the country and both my husband and I worked from home, we felt trapped by some of those decisions. I truly believe your freedom is determined by the options that you have. Money provides those options, but entrepreneurship is the key to freedom because you don't have anyone governing over you so you have different options than most.

Having my child in the public school system where she was subject to thoughts and ideas that were far beyond her scope was of no interest to us as her parents. Now don't get me wrong, we teach and speak to her at the highest level possible, allowing her to ask questions if a concept or conversation doesn't make sense… but to be a part of the public school system with the way of the world right now just wasn't something we wanted knowing how impressionable she is at this young age. So, we decided to opt out. Not only that, but the school system was set up to condition people to become employees, putting them in the highest tax bracket, and if you go to university and end up with a student loan, you're like an ever-giving cash machine as you pay back what you owe plus interest to the government who loaned that money to you in the first place.

We ONLY had the option to pull her from school and move because we worked for ourselves and had figured out how to make a remote income so we could live and work from anywhere. Now, these days, that is quite common and there are so many options for people to do so, but you may be sitting here reading this chapter, feeling pigeonholed into your current circumstance. You're not. You get to make decisions daily to create your future and it's never too late to learn a new skill or pivot.

The other thing we don't talk about in this hustle culture is taking a time-out. What I mean is that we all need time to rest and rejuvenate, but more importantly to take some time to get a balcony view of our lives instead of being in the day-to-day routine. This most often happens in travel when we are able to unplug, rest, relax, and dream.

However, you can also create time and space in your weekly schedule to meditate, journal, evaluate, and adjust course in real-time. Growing up, I thought we needed to have one plan to execute, one big dream, but as I get older, that dream continues to shift and grow. Now, I've realized that all you need to do is make decisions based on what is the next right move for you and your family right now. We have the option to change course and chase adventure. We also have the option to take risks that are aligned with our values, and we only live once, so make sure you do what you truly want so you don't have any regrets.

In October of 2021, we decided to take that risk and take a time out in Mexico, a place both my husband and I loved, where we frequented before having kids and even where we got married. We decided after two devastating miscarriages that we would take a break, rest, and refocus on what we truly wanted our life to look like for us and our little family. Two months later, we burned the boats and sold our home in Canada, embracing this digital nomad life and vowing to figure it out together and do what was best for us instead of what was expected. This wasn't easy. Our family back home was shocked, but we felt like we had started a new life. One we were finally excited about.

This dramatic change was the catalyst that showed us we were capable of anything. With open hearts and open minds, we embraced the adventure and challenge for everything that it is. Just last week, my daughter asked if after Mexico we could live in Italy for a little while, and with a smile on my face I got to say, "I don't see why not." That's the life we are teaching her that she can have. One that is abundant with possibility if you're willing to think outside the box. This is the beauty of being a mompreneur. You get to live your life with purpose and intention and teach your children by example to do the same. I honestly wouldn't want it any other way.

Be Bold. Be Brave. Be Disruptive. You are capable of things far beyond your wildest dreams if you just have the courage to go for it.

Demetriah Annenayah

I AM POWERED BY LOVE
Spiritual Life Coach

https://www.facebook.com/demetriahannenayah
https://www.instagram.com/iampoweredbylove
www.iampoweredbylove.live
www.iampoweredbylove.com

Demetriah Annenayah is a seasoned spiritual coach focused on empowering women. She helps women achieve their entrepreneurial dreams and desires. She has been featured on the Professional Podcast Network and Thrive Network.

Following her surrender to God in 1992, she began helping women develop their life purpose, love relationships, and financial stability. Through personal struggles such as loss, divorce, and economic devastation, she transformed her life. Today, she shares her innovative Soul technology secrets that manifest everything in the Universe.

As a single mother, Demetriah Annenanyah cherishes the joy and love she shares with her daughter. Her personal experiences have equipped her with the wisdom to guide women in overcoming obstacles in love, intimacy, and finances. She empowers women to discover their authentic selves and manifest their dreams through her groundbreaking coaching programs.

To discover more about Demetriah Annenayah and her transformative coaching, visit www.iampoweredbylove.live.

UNLEASH YOUR BUSINESS POTENTIAL WITH SPIRITUAL EMPOWERMENT

By Demetriah Annenayah

Greetings, Beautiful Soul, my fellow mompreneur! Are you ready for a transformative journey into entrepreneurship fueled by love and spiritual empowerment? As moms navigating the intricate dance of business and family, who understands the delicate balance of passion, purpose, and personal well-being better than you? I invite you into a realm where success goes beyond financial gains. This journey is about aligning our ventures with our deepest values and beliefs to carve out time for love, intimacy, and the growth of our income streams, revenue, and capital gains!

My journey into entrepreneurship was anything but conventional, yet it illuminated the transformative power of perseverance and self-belief. As a single mom, I was determined to manifest my purpose and set an example for my daughter. Through spiritual empowerment, I unearthed the keys to sustainable success and fulfillment despite internal struggles and external challenges. I discovered the transformative steps of self-worth, courage, trust, creativity, tenacity, spiritual growth, universal law, and mind-engineering consciousness, shedding toxic beliefs, thoughts, wounds, fears, doubts, and excuses to realize that anything is possible when we transform our internal narrative of who we truly are.

As an entrepreneur, I quickly realized that more than strategic planning is needed to achieve success. Inner alignment, soul wisdom, and spiritual guidance were equally crucial to manifesting joy and achievement in my life. That's why, as a confident spiritual coach and mompreneur, I've devoted my expertise to empowering women to embrace their authentic truth, dare them to turn invisible dreams into tangible manifestations, and encourage them to infuse purpose into their business ventures while inspiring the communities they lead, starting with their families.

In this chapter, we'll discuss the unique challenges that a mompreneur may face. We'll also explore why spiritual coaching is essential in business. How can we overcome internalized fears and meet the needs of our businesses without a solid plan to grow our future revenue streams, love, family, and dreams? Together, we'll delve into the impact of subconscious patterns on our entrepreneurial journeys. We'll embark on a journey of self-discovery and healing to unlock the profound potential within each of us.

The crux of spiritual empowerment lies in identity assessment—a deep dive into our financial and relationship identities. By shedding light on hidden beliefs and emotional blocks, we pave the way for transformative growth and the reward of success. Through practical exercises like deepening our why, reframing our story, and crafting a personal truth statement, we detoxify our minds and align with our highest vision.

Embark on this empowering journey of self-discovery and transformation with me. Let's harness the power of spirituality to redefine success and fulfillment in entrepreneurship. It's time to unlock our true selves and unleash our business potential! Let's navigate the road to becoming conscious mompreneurs together. I invite you to embrace your true self and unlock the transformative potential of spiritual empowerment. Success as a mompreneur is not just about external achievements—it's about cultivating a business that nourishes our spirits and supports our authentic selves.

Self-actualization profoundly impacts the person you become and how your business influences society. As we walk this path, let's imagine how your success can benefit you and shape the legacy you leave for future generations. It's about building a community and a following that can support our children for years to come; a legacy fueled by love, intimacy, and prosperity.

We aren't taught to embrace the infinite truth of divine femininity as a woman and a mom. As a future business leader, this self-awareness of your sacred feminine power, the Yin —a force that births manifestations without force, effortlessly versus belabored, not fueled by aggression but passion, desire, and creativity which is designed to transcend all life — should be at the core of your heart, vision, and dreams. **The Divine Feminine Influence** will not pursue traditional conventional business strategies in the same way as our old toxic masculine dispositions, as we now acknowledge the changes in how we do business, economically, and socially.

The Divine Feminine Influence is taking form in the way we do business here and now, yet we are still approaching it with toxic masculine attributes like aggressive competition, fear-based marketing tactics, and iconic self-branding. To be a brand, we must first unlock the gateway to our truth if we desire others to buy into us, our products, services, and our dreams. The Divine Feminine Influence attracts opportunities, achievements, and partnership alignments and organically grows scalable business ventures.

So, before you put the finishing touches on your business plan, become the plan, the energy, the source of strength and courage, and empower yourself. Your quest to transform your life and future deserves the action of putting you first. Suppose your energy isn't anchored to the dream of your visions. How else will you stand in the face of the many challenges facing women in business today?

The path of a woman entrepreneur is paved with unique challenges from navigating the marketplace and social media landscapes to encountering obstacles in banking and finance. These challenges and lessons often mirror internal struggles and subconscious patterns that can hinder our success and dampen our spirits. It's time to shift gears and embrace a spiritual approach to business and soul-purpose planning that aligns our ventures with our true essence and propels us toward transformative growth.

The more we become aware of the labyrinth of our subconscious patterns that influence our entrepreneurial journeys, the more we realize that our minds are potent reservoirs of beliefs, fears, and insecurities shaped by our experiences and societal conditioning. Unearthing these patterns is the first step towards liberation and empowerment. By shedding light on hidden fears, doubts, and limiting beliefs, we create space for new possibilities, amplify our potential, and pave the way for success on our terms. A mompreneur today must follow this Divine Feminine path.

As women, we face a myriad of challenges beyond our work-from-home space, business locations, or online shops. The digital age presents opportunities and pitfalls, requiring us to navigate social media platforms and online marketing strategies while staying true to our values, voices, and convictions. The financial landscape can be daunting with access to funding and banking services often posing obstacles and limitations to raising capital and lending.

But what of the social media landscape where the barrier to entry in many marketplaces is so low that mompreneurs will not only need help staying in front of their audience but also with creating content in their authentic voice in every new algorithm? How do we rise above these challenges and thrive in our entrepreneurial endeavors? The answer lies in embracing a spiritual paradigm shift that transcends traditional business models and empowers us to lead authentically and purposefully.

Spiritual business coaching offers a transformative approach to entrepreneurship so that you can integrate practical strategies with soulful alignment. For the women who come to me seeking financial security of business ownership, they are able to discover the depths of their vision and passion hidden beneath the illusion of fears, reasons, and justifications as to why they can't pursue their purpose.

The one that encapsulates their full expression as they truly imagine for themselves as opposed to the one they have decided to settle for to make ends meet. It is here that they can give birth to a vision unique to their gifts, talents, abilities, and skills and can infuse every aspect of themselves into their purpose with intention and integrity. This ranges from branding and marketing to customer relations and financial management, all while balancing their family in the alignment of their actions, guided by inner wisdom to cultivate more than a business and a brand. It becomes the very essence that nourishes their souls and infuses their families with new life - which is exactly what I intend to do with you.

To bring tangible manifestations into reality is to harness the power of the Divine Feminine within yourself. As moms, our family depends on every ounce of our energy. Together, we'll achieve the dream of success not just financially but through a holistic balance of self-love, dedication to our sacred dreams, and the pursuit of authenticity over archaic societal beliefs.

The path to self-discovery and spiritual awakening awaits you, and embracing your Divine Feminine sacred self will make you unstoppable. Here are a few exercises that will allow you to engage from deep within yourself, opening up a channel for new consciousness and revelations to flow freely between your heart and mind. By surrendering to this process, you can awaken the essence of your Divine Feminine influence (which is the key to unlocking the true potential of our collective journey as mompreneurs). You should approach this with fierce determination, becoming centered in homeostasis and being open to the honest dialogue of your heart. Let us embrace this journey together and emerge as powerful, enlightened women ready to lead with love and compassion.

Take a moment to meditate and relax. The intention? Uncovering deep insights, overcoming limiting beliefs, and removing emotional barriers that may impede your abundance of love, joy, and success—essential elements for launching your business with purpose and authenticity. Please put the palms of your hands together and center them in front of your heart. The Anjali Mudra, also called the "prayer Mudra," connects the mind, body, soul, and spirit as one whole. Now, gently close your eyes and take ten deep inhalations and exhalations through your nose.

Now, let's dive in!

Exercise 1: Awaken Awareness

Let's begin by exploring our financial and relationship identities. By answering the following five questions, discover if there are any blockages to abundance in the Root Chakra. Keep these blockages from achieving the success of your dreams. Take control of your life and better understand where you stand by answering these questions today.

1. What beliefs do you hold about money and its role in your life?
2. How do you view your worthiness of love and intimacy?
3. Are there any childhood experiences shaping your current relationship with abundance?
4. What societal norms or family beliefs influence your financial decisions?
5. How do your current relationships reflect your beliefs about love and worth?

Welcome to a moment of self-reflection. Allow yourself to resonate with these questions, and let your subconscious reveal its patterns and cycles. Remember, there's no right or wrong answer - only your truth. This exercise will help you release what no longer belongs in your life or business and clarify your values and desires. With this clarity, transformation becomes possible. Take this opportunity to connect with yourself and allow your heart and soul to guide you.

Step 2: Mind Engineer Consciousness to End Toxic Living Patterns

Exercise 1: List 25 words that describe yourself in connection to your business. Allow these words to resonate with your community and reflect your authentic essence.

Exercise 2: Craft a unique value proposition using 150 words. Position yourself authentically within your market, highlighting what sets you apart.

Exercise 3: Now, let's revisit your answers from Step 1 to reflect on who taught you these beliefs and whether they align with your business goals as a mompreneur. How long have you held onto these beliefs, and how often do they manifest in your reality? Are these beliefs truly yours, or are they inherited from others?

Step 3: Reframe Limiting Beliefs into Empowering Intentions

Reframe each of the five beliefs uncovered in Step 1. Transform them into empowering statements that align with your business vision and personal evolution.

Exercise: Crafting your One Statement. I introduce this to my clients between weeks four and five of their soul purpose and entrepreneurial quests with me as a powerful tool that sets up a personal affirmation. There is no such thing as a catch-all affirmation. Sound seeds are personal to your vibration, meaning your heart and mind alignment, that you speak into life force creation from your life force.

Your heart and mind will align with your truth once you're free of counterproductive subconscious beliefs to manifest what you seek to achieve. So, here we intend to apprehend your desires and motivations and encapsulate them into one statement:

Sample Template: "I, [*Your Name*], say yes to my life and all I seek to create in my life and birth as my energy into my business [*insert unique purpose of business*]. Using my unique strengths and values: [*insert five words from your self-description list*]. I allow myself to align with every opportunity for my highest good and for the good of every life I touch with all joy and love.

Say this in your bathroom mirror. Please share your results with me.

Step 4: Time Traveling

Unlock the full potential of your future by embracing your whole self. Remember that healing the wounds of the past is a crucial step towards achieving inner peace and personal growth. We often try to leave the past behind, but we need to learn from it and strengthen our wisdom and resolve. Our values, integrity, and truth are fundamental to our purpose, family, and community. If we try to forget our past hurts and wounds, we continue the cycle of pain and illusion. To transform ourselves, we must release and heal all aspects of our lives as women. I designed a unique time travel capsule exercise with techniques based on clients' individual Chiron Wound patterns and past life experiences to heal emotional wounds and trauma by writing a heartfelt letter to your past self.

Invite her to partake in your newfound wisdom, patience, and vision. Make yourself whole with compassion for yourself and support the past version of your innocence, beauty, and purity. Use that sense of wonder and curiosity to move forward and create a future filled with abundance and purpose:

Dear Past Self,

Sample beginning: I honor you for your journey—the challenges, the lessons, and the growth. Together, we will go on an adventure to places we have longed to go. I will keep you safe, as I have no fear now. I see clearly with the newfound wisdom I have gained and will share with you in loving goodness, a place of our dreams, where love and trust flow freely in exchange for our truth, passions, gifts, and vision. Ever transforming dreams, life, and into reality. [*Don't stop writing until you receive a full release here*]

In the spirit of empowerment and authenticity,

[Your Name Unstoppable Woman]

Please note that if you complete all of these and would like a free mini Sacred Soul Session, please schedule a meeting with me right now to begin your quest for momprenuership, like our example Ari.

Meet Ari, a determined mompreneur who launched her entrepreneurial journey filled with self-doubt and uncertainty. Ari struggled with limiting beliefs about her worthiness and capabilities, stemming from years of familial conditioning and a lack of confidence in her voice, truth, and personal beliefs regarding herself. Despite her passion for her business idea, she hesitated to take bold steps forward, doubting her inner wisdom and disbelief that others would receive her voice. She was used to taking a backseat to the opinions of others, going along to keep the peace.

Through our coaching sessions, Ari confronted her deepest fears and insecurities to acknowledge her unique talents, gifts, and skills in business administration and organization. Ari also possesses innate compassion, love, and nurturing support for those around her. Together, we explored her subconscious patterns and identified underlying beliefs that held her back. Ari discovered the profound impact of self-love and authenticity on her entrepreneurial path, which changed her direction.

One pivotal moment came when Ari realized that her struggles with expressing her truth or standing in her convictions were rooted in childhood experiences and familial expectations. She bravely reframed her limiting beliefs and values for herself into transmuting self-worth expression and forms of her creativity which strengthened her position to speak her truth or shrink her worthiness. The more she grew, the more Ari began taking on other areas that were dear to her heart.

Ari began taking on her Divine Feminine influence with grace and transcendence, allowing her gifts, talents, and abilities to shine. It wasn't long before she was attracting opportunities to showcase her growth and be received by her peers in her industry. She attracted new clients and opportunities effortlessly, confidently embodying her unique value proposition. Ari's transformation inspired her to lead authentically, nurturing her business from a place of love and purpose.

Today, Ari is a shining success story that serves as a beacon of hope for fellow mompreneurs. With a professional career of her own making and a second successful business partnership with her husband, Ari now travels around the world with the security of a loving family and a new soul tribe to support her scaling business.

She continues to thrive, demonstrating that self-belief and inner alignment are essential keys to fulfilling one's soul purpose and abundance of love, intimacy, and financial gains.

Enter our second example, Summer - a hard-working mompreneur struggling with recurring relationship patterns affecting her business growth and expansion. Summer grappled with identity issues rooted in past relationships which led to challenges in aligning with abundance and financial support in her business because she always believed that no one would ever truly be there for her. Her business suffered from her issues of rejection and abandonment.

During our coaching quest, Summer bravely confronted her relationship patterns, recognizing their impact on her entrepreneurial endeavors. Together, we delved into her subconscious beliefs about love, intimacy, and money, focusing on each to dismantle their energetic disruptions. Summer challenged herself to create beliefs that aligned with who she was becoming.

Summer's breakthrough came when she realized that her struggles with money and relationships were interconnected. She could love herself by reframing her beliefs countering how much she could and should earn as an artist as she began loving herself more fully. Summer is a talented and gifted artist. Her ability to bring the best out of others inspires her craft; when Summer paints your canvas, she helps others unlock new levels of confidence and authenticity.

Through practical exercises, techniques, and formulas created exclusively for her pilgrimage, Summer crafted a powerful One Statement, aligning her newly found confidence with her business vision and personal growth. In doing so, she realized she had the power to nourish herself to peace with the new version of herself, shedding old stories and societal beliefs that no longer served her.

As Summer healed her relationship patterns, her business flourished. A client asked her to do a Divine Feminine body painting retreat; the rest is history. She attracted clients who resonated with her holistic approach to embodying their Divine Feminine influence and found a voice and expression of herself that she knew existed. Summer's journey exemplifies the consciously-expanding power of self-awareness and healing in mompreneurship.

Summer's success story today inspires fellow mompreneurs to prioritize self-love and authenticity. She continues to embrace her Divine Feminine influence, demonstrating that inner alignment is the cornerstone of sustainable business success.

Let me take you on a journey through my own experiences—a modern-day odyssey of spiritual enlightenment that started over 48+ years ago. You see, I've always had this nagging feeling that I was meant for something greater, but accepting God's calling for my life? Well, that seemed like a job for someone much more put-together than me. Self-love? Oh boy, that was my biggest lesson to learn for many years.

I possess spiritual gifts and abilities, sure, but back then talking openly about them was like being a bull in a room full of china—awkward and isolating. While I could see my purpose clearly, I was also acutely aware of what others were here to do according to their soul's contract. I could see and communicate with crossed-over loved ones. Hear people's thoughts as they were thinking them, see future world events, and the personal outcomes of people's next decisions. Who in the world could I talk to about all of this without appearing to me absolutely looney in the 80s?

But the biggest question of all later, once my daughter was born, was how could I possibly turn this into a business and serve others authentically when I was too scared to even share what I knew, saw, and heard with others?

In my quest for clarity, confidence, and self-compassion, I plunged headfirst into several business ventures as a business consultant, mentor, realtor, and property management family company owner, each becoming my playground for refining business ethics and practices.

Oh, I encountered failures and made mistakes—lots of them! But each misstep was a stepping stone to spiritual expansion.

These experiences taught me the magic of aligning my spiritual beliefs with my entrepreneurial endeavors. I mean, I was changing my subconscious belief systems before it was cool before people knew what chakras, crystals, and neurotransmitters were! I was the poster child for all Indigo Children! Picture this: friends and family raising their eyebrows, doubting God's ability to elevate my life through business ventures. Bless their hearts! I've been an outcast all my life. So, I embraced the crazy.

But you know what? My purpose wasn't just about building successful businesses—it was about empowering and supporting women to manifest love, relationships, financial security, and prosperity.

One of my greatest triumphs was finally seeing myself the way God sees me—a feat only I could accomplish. I had to forgive myself for seeking external validation when I had this precious treasure within me, bestowed by the divine. So, I'm passionate about guiding other women, especially mothers, to theirs!

I embarked on a journey of nurturing, nourishing, and feeding my soul while forgiving those whose karmic contracts involved pushing my buttons—and boy, did they push! But I never backed down from my spiritual beliefs; they're etched in my heart.

As I gained more trust in the universe's power to manifest and the wisdom to heal emotional and physical ailments, I took confident steps forward. Today, I guide my clients through their journeys, sharing personal lessons learned—the struggles with guilt and shame as a mom, the challenges of navigating business decisions, and the intuitive risks that scaled operations.

I learned that guilt and shame are not meant to hold us back but to propel us forward with resilience and determination. Taking sovereign possession of my spiritual gifts and calling revealed a profound truth: our greatest challenges often catalyze our most significant victories.

So here I am, a living testament to the transformative power of embracing divine purpose. True success isn't just about financial gains; it's about embodying authenticity and aligning with our soul's calling. Because, my friends, fortune indeed favors the bold, and the secret to all this sauce is in universal timing.

I celebrate each of you and the radiant beauty you exude as you navigate the steps of mompreneurship. You wear it well, beautiful souls! But let's pause for a moment to do some deep cleaning of our subconscious closets before we birth our visions and dreams into the world. Many of my clients have found me just when they're at the threshold of throwing in the towel, and I'm here to tell you: don't give up, for your breakthrough may be just around the corner.

Now, let's allow this truth to sink in—resonate with your Divine Feminine influence and the revolutionary energy it holds for your entrepreneurial ventures and personal life. Take a moment to return to the mini-exercises within this chapter. We've explored the essential balance of nurturing your soul's purpose while growing successful businesses—not through sweat equity and brute force, but by infusing feminine power and intuition into every endeavor.

It's about connecting with yourself in sacred ways that lead to increased business success, deeper love and relationships, enhanced intimacy, and strengthened emotional bonds with your family and children.

Embracing your true self is not just a step—it's a courageous leap toward unlocking your highest potential. Honor your spiritual gifts and wisdom; allow them to guide you in business and life. Challenge yourself to take the lessons and insights you've gained to heart. See what inner wisdom arises within you and begin aligning your true essence with your business, shedding outdated beliefs, and stepping confidently into your purpose.

Here are actionable steps to support you on this transformative journey:

- **Daily Mirror Manifestations:** Dedicate time each day to connect with your inner wisdom during your morning beauty routine. As you apply your makeup or care for your skin, say your One Statement Affirmation out loud ten times. Feel the resonance within you; let your intuition guide you to a clear "yes" or "no" response.

- **Continued Entrepreneurial Evolution:** Each of you is blessed with unique visions and dreams aligned with your soul's purpose on this planet. Seek out sisterhood mentors and coaches who resonate with your journey. Together, we evolve and thrive.

- **Team Building:** Surround yourself with like-minded individuals who uplift and inspire you. Consider the trio of third-party people you'll need: a treasurer with CMSA designation, a social media coach, and a spiritual business coach. These allies will support your growth and wealth.

- **Actionable Steps:** Infuse intention and authenticity into your business strategy. Let spiritual principles guide your branding, marketing, and customer interactions. Success is not just about external achievements; it's about the depth of connection you cultivate within yourself and others. Trust in the power of the Divine Feminine to lead you towards abundance in all areas of your life.

Do not take yourself too seriously. Embrace imperfection, celebrate your wins, remember your why, and always remember that you are the one in control of your thoughts, beliefs, and outcomes. Permit yourself to express your truth!

Thank you for embarking on this empowering adventure with me. May you shine brightly, embodying the essence of your Divine Feminine influence and manifesting your dreams with grace and authenticity.

Here's to your success, joy, and unwavering connection to the sacred within you.

With love and divine light,
Demetriah Annenayah

Dina Moench

Unite the Road Less Traveled Inc.
Family Entrepreneurship Event Planner

https://www.linkedin.com/in/dina-moench-a7b9172a/
https://www.facebook.com/dina.cioffi.1
https://www.instagram.com/dinamoench/

I've decided to take my role as Mompreneur and become an event planner where I am creating a Family Entrepreneur Experience on board cruise ships. I would love for the term Familypreneurship to take flight alongside Mompreneur. I am a mom of three boys Jason, Charlie, and Jack and I married my high school sweetheart Tim. Together we live in Cherry Hill in a really fun filled life adventure. I love writing and dream of being a NY Times Bestselling author. My favorite thing to do is spend time with my family! I love hiking, camping, traveling, and making food together. My dream is to go on long trips where I spend my days writing ideas that I am able to brainstorm with my kids.

FROM MOMPRENUER TO FAMILYPRENUER

By Dina Moench

Mompreneur is such a glorious word. It combines my absolute favorite things in the world – being a mom with entrepreneurship, the unique ability to design what you want and bring it into existence. I am so proud when I have something exit my brain space and become a tangible item that I can show the world. My kids especially love to encourage me, and for that, I am entirely grateful. I encourage them as well, and that dynamic has been so uplifting to me. With all the opinions in the world, the ones that truly matter to me are those of my kids. Each time I talk to my kids as a mompreneur, they encourage me! Each time I talk to them about their ideas, I encourage them.

I've decided to take my role as mompreneur and become an event planner where I am creating a Family Entrepreneur Experience. I would love for the term "familypreneurship" to take flight alongside "mompreneur." My event will take place January 16-20th on the Carnival Paradise Cruise leaving from Tampa, Florida. I'm so excited for this event for familypreneruship bonding and promoting financial literacy. I plan to host one or two cruises annually and would love for anyone reading this book to consider coming along for the journey!

Here is a little about my story and how I got to where I am today. I set a goal for myself: I wanted to be an accredited investor by the time I was 30 years old with a net worth of one million dollars. I did not hit that goal. However, on my 30th birthday, I had one son on my lap who was one year old, and I was pregnant with my second son. I thought to myself, this feeling of being a mom is worth more than a million dollars, for sure! When my kids were three and four years old, I decided to make my Instagram handle "Moms.of.millionaires" because I wanted to interview moms who raised kids to have financial freedom and financial peace combined together. I wanted to use the Instagram account to ask others who had financial knowledge to educate people on financial literacy and do it by interviewing wealthy people and posting stories about their journey online. I wanted to interview moms of millionaires to see what they did to raise their kids. I then had a sense of inner peace about missing my goal of being a millionaire by the time I was 30. I told my kids that instead of becoming a millionaire on my own, I thought it would be a more fun and educational experience for my kids if we built our generational wealth together. It is estimated that 70% of wealthy families will lose their wealth by the second generation, and 90% will lose it by the third. How do you fall within the percentage of families that can keep their wealth?

Walt Disney has been an inspiration in my life from the time I was a young girl, watching Disney movies, to becoming an adult and understanding that his first venture flopped. The lessons he learned created the foundation of the Disney empire and all that it stands for today. "To Walt, 'plus' was a verb—an action word—signifying the delivery of more than what his customers paid for or expected to receive. He constantly challenged his Imagineers to see what was possible, and then take it a step further … and then a step beyond that."

The idea of "plussing" is one that we use in my house often. When someone has a good idea, we say let's plus it. Then, we add more ideas of how we can make a great idea even better. For example, if we want to go on a picnic, we could plus the idea by adding a frisbee and a hike afterward, and then we could add buying lunch for someone who doesn't have a lot of money. We could drop a picnic off for them so they can go on their own adventure. Each time we "plus," we decide if the idea would add to the journey. Each time I hear "plussing," I make a mental note of how many ways Walt Disney has impacted my life.

"All our dreams can come true if we have the courage to pursue them," is a famous quote by Walt Disney. I want my kids to have the courage to pursue all their dreams. It is important for me as a mompreneur to lead by example. I want to pursue all my own dreams, support my kids' dreams, and be uplifting about how we can encourage each other along the journey.

More importantly than wealth, I focus on how I can teach my children to have inner peace. Inner peace to me is what a mompreneur should specialize in. It's not about the money; it's about what the money can do in your life. My life has never been about money. It's about experiencing life to the fullest that it has to offer each and every single day.

So, when I made my Moms of Millionaires logo, I showed it to my kids. I took them with me to an embroidery shop, and I paid $47 for them to put the logo on a bookbag that I carry around with me. My kids thought, "My mom is a mom of millionaires, so I'm going to be a millionaire." I didn't actually say that. I was just trying to be cute with my Instagram handle. Once I realized the power of thought, I made sure that my bookbag that had Moms of Millionaires on it with my name (Dina) on it was present often.

One of my favorite moments was when my seven-year-old took my bookbag and made me a shirt that had the same logo. He surprised me with it and brought tears to my eyes. What once started as an Instagram handle morphed into a backpack with my name on it, then turned into my kids saying, "I'm going to be a millionaire because my mom is 'Moms of Millionaires.'"

My kids and I, before bed, use a confidence-building app called "Legends" created by a phenomenal entrepreneur named Sunny Caberal. "Legends" taught us to do box breathing when we feel stressed about anything. Sometimes, I'm not really sure whether or not the things I'm doing with my kids are being absorbed. Fast forward a few weeks to a trip that I was on with my three sons where I lost my rental car keys. I looked everywhere. In all of our luggage, our hotel room, and the entire rental car. There wasn't a place that I could think of to look where I hadn't already looked. Then, a thought popped into my head. We ate at Wawa, and I threw away a bag of trash. What if I threw away the rental car keys? We looked everywhere else and couldn't find them, so I went to check the trash can. When I realized the hotel emptied the trash can by the front door where I threw in the trash, I wondered if they had an onsite dumpster. So, I went to the hotel front desk, and my five-year-old son Charlie said, "Mommy, you seem stressed. Do you think box breathing will help right now?" He helped me to do box breathing, and it absolutely did help. My keys were in the dumpster.

My familypreneurship cruise has been something that my family and I are planning together. We love to talk about and brainstorm special guests that we want to come on board. We plan to make this an annual event, and when I asked my son what I should write about in the mompreneur book, he said, "You should write about how in 50 years, when we have done 50 years of cruises, it started by planning the first one." I think those are wise words, and I'm so proud of all three of my sons. It's an honor to be their mom and an even greater honor to be their mompreneur.

My phrase to my kids is, "Mommy wants to help you get everything you want in the world."

Sometimes my kids will misquote me and say, "Mommy, you said, 'You want to give me everything I want in the world.'"

I gently tell them they have a few words off, and it makes a difference. "I didn't say I want to **give** you everything you want in the world... I said, 'I want to **help** you get everything you want in the world.'" I tell them, "I want YOU to first decide what you want. Then I want to HELP you get what you want, NOT give you what you want." I tell them when they want something, they should come to me and ask for my help to get it. My help comes in many forms. From creating lemonade stands to helping them buy what they want with earned money, to printing out a photo for a vision board, to sometimes buying it and sending them on a scavenger hunt to find it.

For me, creating a vision board with my kids has been one of my greatest experiences, and I highly recommend it! We got a large foam board and printed out pictures - one for each member of the family. Then, we use gold stickers when one of the things on our vision board comes true. I love that my kids aren't afraid to ask for things both big and small. I get to see what is inside their minds. I also LOVE having a default answer to anything that I am not in a position to get them.

I can always say, "Let's print out a picture of the thing you want, and we can put it on your vision board." It allows us to have far less conflict and they get a gold star when they eventually get what they want. It's a lesson in delayed gratification plus advanced planning and goal setting.

My biggest joy is my own inner peace, which I feel great about. My days are filled with a majority of inner peace. Mompreneurship hasn't been a straight-line path for me. There have been a lot of financial ups and downs. A lot of emotional ups and downs too. But now, I view it as a roller coaster of fun instead of "ups and downs." I have gained the perspective that the ups and the downs are equally important in the journey. I'm as open as I can be with my kids about my journey and all that it entails.

I found a canvas at a thrift store with a saying that I love. It says, "When life hands you lemons, make apple juice and leave the world wondering how you did it." It's in my living room, and I think that is a huge part of my inner peace. Some people are just happy. The world can hand them whatever it wants and their default emotion is happiness. Even when people are sad, they can be happy that they are feeling sad. That sad emotion comes with the feeling that what they are feeling sad about is worthy of that emotion, and therefore actually makes them happy.

To my fellow mompreneurs – I hope you gain some insight in this book that we are not alone. We are raising the next generation of humans. No matter what our kids do, I hope for them to find their own inner peace. If we teach them to do that, we will live in a more peaceful world. So, from me to all the other mompreneurs out there, "When life hands you lemons, make apple juice and leave the world wondering how you did it."

To all the kids out there, I've asked my sons what to say. From Jason, age seven:

> "I think it is nice being a kid. Since my mom is planning the cruise she won't have to go out to work so much and we can go on cruises for free."

From Charlie, age five:

> "I like planning the cruise together because you don't have to leave to go to work so much, and we will have fun on the cruise, and we can invite our best friends to go on the cruise with us."

From my infant son, Jack:

> Laughter and smiles.

Ksenia Droben

CEO of Ksenia Droben Matchmaking

https://www.linkedin.com/in/ksenia-droben-911289148/
https://www.facebook.com/ksenia.droben
https://instagram.com/kseniadroben.agency
www.droben-matchmaking.com
www.bridespb.com

Ksenia Droben, a distinguished figure in international matchmaking and dating coaching, is renowned for her multifaceted contributions to the field. Beyond her role as a matchmaker and coach, she serves as a dynamic host of both online and offline events, fostering connections among singles in interactive and engaging settings.

As a certified matchmaker, Ksenia brings a wealth of knowledge and expertise to her practice, ensuring her clients receive the highest standard of service and support. Her credentials and experience make her a sought-after speaker at international conferences, where she shares insights and best practices in the realm of relationships and matchmaking.

Moreover, Ksenia's influence extends to television, where she has made appearances as a trusted TV-matchmaker, offering guidance and expertise to viewers seeking love and companionship. Through her diverse roles and platforms, Ksenia Droben continues to shape and enrich the world of matchmaking, leaving a lasting impact on countless lives worldwide.

WHAT YOU TRULY DESIRE CAN BECOME REALITY

By Ksenia Droben

Being a mompreneur in today's world can be very challenging. Mompreneur refers to a mother who is also an entrepreneur.

On one hand, women want to utilise their skills and talents to fulfil their dreams and mission. On the other hand, women are the only ones who can bear children, and the expectations placed on parents are constantly increasing.

During my childhood, which was a happy and screen-free time spent with friends and books, my mother would guide and entertain me without any hesitation. She had to survive, and I had to organize my life and activities alone. Nowadays, parents are responsible for managing their children's time, homework, hobbies, and well-being.

I believe most mothers can relate to this.

Currently, I am a successful, international matchmaker and dating coach, having helped thousands of couples. However, it was not always this way. Have you ever had the feeling of thinking you are winning, but in reality, you were losing?

In November 2013, my ex-husband announced that he no longer wanted to stay with us in Germany and wished to return to Russia. At the time, we had just purchased a house with a large mortgage and had four children, ranging in age from three to seventeen years old. Only three months after buying the expensive house, he decided to leave and 'search for himself.' I was utterly shocked and unable to describe the depth of my feelings. Since he no longer has any contact with the children, I cannot find any excuses for this behaviour. In my opinion, while you don't have to love or live with your spouse, children are not toys that can be discarded. Am I right?

Additionally, I experienced a double loss as I lost my job as a matchmaker at the same time despite being very good at it. I provided prompt and straightforward guidance and tailored my language to suit different individuals. However, the loss of my family and husband shattered my self-confidence. I felt inadequate coaching others on relationships when I couldn't maintain my own. I was burdened with guilt towards my children and unable to continue working which immediately impacted my financial situation. Firstly, I could not stay in the office for too long as my children were waiting for me at home. This included picking them up from kindergarten, shopping, cooking, and other activities. Despite this, I was unable to work and had to stop answering calls and client requests. I needed to conserve my energy to maintain my mental well-being.

I remember the moment when I was sitting with a piece of paper, writing down the amount of money I had in different accounts: 50 Euros on PayPal, 35 Euros on my bank card, etc. I had to put money together to pay my mortgage and taxes, and feed my kids.

To accumulate some income, I started renting out a room on Booking.com. It was a nightmare for the family. They had to check in and out at all hours of the day, deal with annoying, loud, and complaining guests, and clean up after two groups of guests in a rush.

The breaking point for me was when I had to clean up after a very messy guest and said to myself, 'Enough.' I am a woman with two higher education degrees, my own company, and a lot of knowledge and experience. Is cleaning toilets after messy clients really part of my job?

To alleviate my mental distress, I turned to dating and created a profile on Tinder. Initially, it was a welcome distraction, but I soon realized that I was not treating my dates fairly by seeing multiple people in a day. I did not remember their names as it was unnecessary. I simply met them for coffee and waited for the next candidate, hoping for some magic to happen. So I was very good at dating and had many dates in a short period of time, but at the same time, I was very bad at dating because it was just a distraction. I remember the moment when I sat and listened to some endless story and just wondered why I was wasting my time here.

I do not believe in magic or pink unicorns but I found my rescue in science. Fortunately, I decided to sign up for dating coach certification to gain more background and data for my job. After 12 weeks of lessons and homework, my life changed completely. At the time of my education, I had been working in my profession for almost 20 years, and very successfully. I gave my couples good advice that helped them find love and build relationships. But I never asked myself why it worked this way and not another way. And only a scientific approach allowed me to explain what was happening. Have you ever heard about the science behind first impressions? Or how to choose the right romantic partner? Or how important love is for happy, strong, and healthy relationships? Or how to get rid of emotional baggage?

If you want to know more, ask me! I would be honored to share this knowledge with you.

My business has completely changed! All of my actions were based not only on my personal experience and knowledge but also on scientific research. I completed my dating coach certification, obtained a matchmaker's certification, and joined a society of experienced matchmakers to exchange ideas and best practices.

More importantly, I met my partner despite being busy with my job and having kids of my own. Dominic is an amazing man who is very supportive and understanding. My 'aha-moment' with him was when he asked me why I never mention my kids' names, only referring to them as 'my son' or 'my daughter,' I hadn't even noticed it but being a single mom meant being careful not to overload men you meet with too much information about your kids.

For three years, we lived in different countries and visited each other as much as possible. During this time, I gained insight into how my clients felt when their partners were in other countries. However, the next challenge was COVID-19 which meant no flights or travel. As an international matchmaker, my clients needed to fly and travel to meet each other. It felt like the end of the world for me because I couldn't find any way to earn money when people couldn't travel.

Nevertheless, where there is a will, there is a solution. The internet and videos have become our new reality. My clients have started doing various activities online such as cooking together over video, practicing yoga, learning foreign languages, going on dates, drawing, and even learning dance steps. To adapt to these changes, I have started hosting online live webinars, singles parties, and dating marathons. As a result, my agency has evolved beyond being just a matchmaking company; we are now friends. This has brought me closer to my clients, and they try to help me wherever they can.

At some point between two waves of COVID, I made the decision to move to London with my two youngest children to live with my partner. Although he is not their father, he spends more time with them than I do and takes better care of their school life.

As for me, I have built my own dating empire where singles feel comfortable and welcome. I do things differently from all other matchmakers in my agency, and that's okay. I want to feel happy and fulfilled in my job and personal life.

Although I am content with my private life, I have also started feeling more comfortable in this foreign country. I have even learned how to drive on the opposite side of the road.

I believe that anyone can achieve their goals with the right skill set and mindset, regardless of age, family situation, skin colour, or background. If you truly desire something, you can make it a reality.

Every person and every professional has moments when things are going badly and the mood is at zero. It is then that I begin to look at the photographs of the couples who have met thanks to me - I look at their happy faces, their smiles, their beautiful children. And I understand that these couples are the goal of all my work. No matter how difficult and challenging it may be at times, my team and I have a purpose. And that goal is to help great people build great relationships.

I am often asked how my work and my children fit together. Both children and work have accepted each other. I can attend a professional conference and take one of my children with me. Or I can host an event and the children help me translate or prepare the event. Or I can discuss my clients' situations with the children and help my children build their personal lives.

One of my main principles is to get maximum enjoyment out of everything I do. So, most of the time, I don't just carry out my responsibilities at home and at work; I also enjoy what's going on around me.

LaTasha Henry

Empowerment Journey/Empowering YOU
Certified Life Coach

https://www.linkedin.com/in/latasha-h-279892b2/
https://www.facebook.com/groups/1332654857099489/user/100001
454005921/
https://www.instagram.com/empowering_you3/
https://thelifecoachschool.com/big-goals-workshop/

As a certified life coach with seven years of experience, I specializes in empowering individuals to navigate the complexities of relationships— be it family, self, work, business, or marriage. Drawing from personal triumphs over PTSD and the challenges of motherhood, I founded Empowerment Journey, a beacon of support offering mental health resources and transformative workbooks. My approach is deeply empathetic, rooted in my own journey, and dedicated to helping others overcome obstacles and achieve their goals. Balancing the roles of a life coach, business owner, wife and mother of three, I embody the resilience and dedication I instill in my clients. This book is a testament to my belief in the power of self-discovery and the strength that lies in shared experiences.

FROM SHADOWS TO SUNSHINE

By LaTasha Henry

As a child, I walked through life with pure innocence, until one day that innocence was prematurely taken from me, and playing house was no longer fun. You see, I was around nine years old when the unspeakable happened, leaving scars that no child should ever bear. All I can remember feeling was sadness because a game I once loved playing every day became a game that involved new rules, rules I didn't understand, and left me feeling confused and uncomfortable. Yet, even in the darkest moments, a flicker of resilience burned within me. As a teenager, I had people around me who didn't have good intentions and would make up stories about things I had supposedly done.

I believe they got most excited when it came to dealing with punishment and coming up with the most ridiculous things for me to do. I remember one time I had to rake big landscaping rocks from one side of the yard to the other. They just stood there with their friends, drinking beer and laughing. I asked for gloves to help me keep from getting blisters but I was told we didn't have any. You can imagine how hard it was to do this, especially with a rake that kept bending.

I think the worst was when I was 16 and my mom had just bought me the car I had been wanting. Well, Dick (my step-dad at the time) decided he was going to pick me up one day from school drunk. He had his friend George in the car with him; bottles of liqueur were all over the backseat. I asked if I could drive but of course, I was told no. Dick said that he wanted to show me what my car could do. I said I didn't want to know, but of course, that didn't matter. He was set on showing me and trying to look like this big badass in front of George. I remember hearing Dick say how fast we were going, and the last speed I heard was 90mph.

I noticed there was a car coming and we were going to be in this curve at the same time. There was no way, going that fast, that we were going to make that curve without wrecking, I closed my eyes and just held onto the door handle. I hear George say "Oh shit," and Dick said "Fuck." The car flipped and I was just praying for it all to be over with soon. We flipped three times and landed on the roof then slid for what seemed like forever. Finally, the car stopped and I screamed, trying to kick out the window while Dick and George were just worried about the alcohol bottles in the car and Dick getting a DUI. Dick told George to get rid of the bottles and then told me that if anyone asked, I was the one driving.

I can remember screaming and telling Dick, "I can't believe you did this." It was at that time that a man came and pulled me out of the car. He kept asking me if I was ok and walked me to his car so I could sit down. The cops came and started asking questions. I could hear Dick tell them that I was driving, and when they came over to question me, they wouldn't allow Dick to be there. They asked if I was driving, and I just kept looking down at the man who pulled me out of the car. He told them that he pulled from the passenger side, so he didn't think it was possible for me to be the driver.

I was the only one taken to the hospital. I remember just wanting my mom. I was so scared. I think the ER staff knew there was more going on because they told Dick nobody but my mom was allowed to come into the area I was being looked at. I had no idea what was happening. There were so many doctors and nurses all asking me different questions and placing these wires on me to hook me up to various machines, telling me everything was going to be ok. I was crying for my mom, and they reassured me that she was on her way. It was then I heard my mom yelling my name. I felt her grab my hand, asking if I was ok. For the first time since being in a car wreck, I felt safe and calm. Something about my mom's voice just made me feel like I was going to be ok.

The rest of my family started showing up at some point. They decided Dick could come back into my room. All he cared about was making sure he told everyone I was driving and that I didn't tell the truth. My daddy knew something about his story didn't make sense, so he took Dick out of my room so my mom could talk to me. She walked over, looked at me, and said, "You weren't driving, were you? Dick was." I just started crying, and she tried to comfort me the best she could with me being hooked up to all the equipment plus a neck brace. It wasn't easy to really get to me, shortly after this my mom divorced Dick.

I now see the world through different lenses, changed by things that were out of my control. I tell myself this all must have had a reason, but will I ever find the reason why? I turned 18 and decided to take a job that allowed me to travel and visit most of the States. While on the road, I learned a lot and saw things I never dreamed were a thing. Making memories and building relationships that would last a lifetime, not realizing soon I would soon find the reason why.

While on the road, I met this guy who later became the man of my dreams. So protecting and loving, he kept me safe. I just knew I found my forever person. As time went by, Jay and I decided it was time to get off the road and start a different journey. We were home only a month when we found out our lives were going to change forever. I was so scared. *How can I care for a baby? I don't have time for this. I'm only 19.* Jay was so happy and kept telling me we would be fine, just trying to ease my mind. The next nine months flew by, and soon I was holding my beautiful baby girl. I held her tight, thanking God for allowing me to have this amazing gift. All my fears and worries vanished. All I cared about was keeping my baby safe. I was what they call a "helicopter mom," not letting anyone hold my baby or not wanting her to get dirty because "she's perfect and I will keep her that way."

My mom was watching her one day, and when I came to pick her up, I saw my baby playing in a mud puddle. I was so upset all I could see was mud all over her and her clothes. My mom told me it was ok as she took her and gave her a bath while telling me she had fun. I definitely didn't see the fun in playing in the mud, getting all dirty and gross. Much to my surprise, I would soon learn that mud would be the least of my concerns.

I had a doctor's appointment. You know, the one where they refill your birth control and make sure everything is going well. I had decided that I no longer wanted the shot; it made me gain weight, and that was nothing I needed help with. When you go to the doctor's for birth control, you have to do a pregnancy test before they give you a refill. Knowing that I was on the shot, I just knew I was in the clear. As I walked out with new birth control in hand, I heard the nurse call me back in. I was very confused because I had everything, so I didn't leave anything behind. The doctor came in, pointed to my birth control, and stated, "You can't take that, your test was positive."

There was no way - they definitely got my test mixed up or read it wrong. The doctor reassured me there was no mix-up. I was having a baby. I didn't know how I was going to tell anyone, let alone how I was going to deal with it. I was just learning how to be a mom and getting a routine. I got to my mom's house to pick up my baby. She asked what the doctor said. I say nothing. I still don't know how but she looked at me and told me I was pregnant. I started crying, saying I didn't want to talk about it, and I still needed to tell Jay. I roleplayed in my head how I was going to tell him, thinking about what he was going to say.

As I got home, I saw he had already gotten home from work already. I started crying, not knowing what to say or how to tell him. Everything I had just practiced went away. He asked, "What's wrong?"

I just blurted out, "I'm pregnant."

He started laughing while saying, "That's what is wrong?" He was happy and hoping for a boy while I hoped for a girl because I had everything for a girl. We went to the doctor's to get everything confirmed. We later would learn we were having a boy. It wasn't long after that I would be holding the boy who would carry my heart in his hands. He was so handsome and cute it didn't take long for me to

I realized that one of the best feelings ever was looking into the eyes of my precious baby boy, knowing he would hold my heart in the palm of his hands forever. My life was perfect with a girl and a boy. How lucky I was to have the best of both worlds. What I didn't know was that time really does change everything. My babies became toddlers in what seemed like overnight. I just needed time to slow down. My life as I knew it was about change, and what I thought was my forever would now just be an end to what I considered to be the perfect little life. At 24, life dealt me another cruel hand.

As I found myself sitting and crying in the shower, trying to understand why a man would want to do something like this to anyone and praying that my kids would never experience this kind of pain, The pain of someone forcing themselves onto you. I asked God to give me strength and guidance to overcome yet another horrible experience. I refused to let it define me. Instead, I found strength in my vulnerability, learning that survival wasn't just about enduring—it was about thriving. It was at that moment that I found the "why," and I realized that everything I had experienced was all to make and shape me into a better mom. I had knowledge that others may not have had, using it as a learning tool to protect and guide my kids along the way while someday being able to help others as well.

During this time, Jay made some horrible choices that would take him away. Once again, I was left feeling like I didn't know what I was going to do. Living with nightmares became just another normal thing. Dealing with panic attacks and being afraid to leave my home, not being able to work and take care of my kids. Having no income left me not being able to pay my bills, and everything we had worked for was being taken away. I could feel my world crumbling. Being a single mom was never my plan, but there I was, having two toddlers looking for me to get by and care for their every need. Having no clue what I was going to accomplish this.

I packed up my kids and moved in with my mom. My kids couldn't understand why their daddy wasn't coming home, and we had to move. I tried to explain the best I could, praying to God to send me the right words. I was always honest with my kids. I just tried to find words that they would understand. It took a while but we did finally get into a routine that seemed to work for everyone. Learning to be a single mom was a lot harder than expected while juggling my work schedule with their school schedule, not to mention the doctor appointments and play dates that also had to be figured out. It was during this time that I became dependent on my kids. I needed them to feel safe, and I looked to them to keep going no matter how hard it got. I didn't have a choice but to get up and keep going. I was all they had, and I got one shot. There are no redoes, and I have to get it right, if not for me then at least for them. I used to always say that I didn't care if I failed at everything else as long as I was a good mom; that's all that matters.

I was a single mother for seventeen years, juggling the joys and trials of parenthood while making sure my children never wore the same scars I did. I was judged, doubted, and received some horrible messages from those who should've been supporting me the most. "How are you going to raise two kids on your own?" they would ask. Some said we would just be another family in the system, and my kids would be statistics. Calls would go unanswered for fear we were calling to ask for help. I tried so hard to be strong and keep my kids from hearing the judgment and reminding them every day how loved and strong they are. I worked hard for long hours while taking on the demands of my role as a public safety officer. It was a life of service, protecting others while silently nursing my own wounds.

In 2018, my kids were now 12 and 13 years old, and I found out that God had yet another surprise. I was having a baby. Yikes. Having procured a few years back, being told I wouldn't be able to carry another baby ever again, and being on birth control, this was something I definitely was not expecting to ever happen. I found myself angry asking God why, knowing that I would see the reason soon.

Sometimes it just takes a little longer to see the reason. The doctors were concerned that I wouldn't be able to carry my baby and they were worried about the health of my baby because I was on birth control. I decided it would be best if I only shared with family until we were in the clear, and I knew if I was going to be able to carry a healthy baby. As time went on and I was waiting to see how my body was going to respond, I got hit with news that would turn my world upside down. I learned the heartbreaking news that my daddy had brain cancer, and they didn't think he would make it past Christmas. I was completely devastated. I was a daddy's girl and I was his baby girl. I was going to navigate life without him, and what about his grandbaby he would never see? As time moved on, I was finally told that I would be able to carry and that my baby looked very healthy. I can remember one of the things my daddy would say. "I'm going to make it to see my grandbaby." When he would say that, I would agree while also thinking, even if in spirit he will be sure he sees he's his grandbaby.

Christmas came and went, and my daddy was still there, anxiously waiting for his grandbaby to arrive. March came and I was in and out of the hospital. I couldn't keep my blood pressure down, and the baby's heart continued to spike. The doctors decided it was best to stay in the hospital so they could monitor me and the baby more closely. It was late in the middle of the night when I started to not feel right. So, I rang for my nurse who came and took my vitals. She said my blood pressure was very high and so was the baby's heart rate, and she needed to call the doctor. The doctor made the call to do a C-section because the baby had to come out. The risk was too high for me to keep carrying. My kids, mom, and stepdad were all there but my daddy couldn't be because of the cancer. I Facetimed him before they took me back, and he said everything would be fine, "I love you."

My mom went with me while my kids and stepdad waited in my room. I could feel them touching and pulling on my stomach. It's really amazing how hard they have to pull and stretch your stomach. I mean, obviously, I couldn't see anything, but man I could feel it. I lay there, waiting to hear something, and soon I heard what sounded like a water main breaking and all this pressure in my belly started going away. Then it felt like they were pulling my organs out. It was the worst feeling ever. I then felt my baby was out and like I could breathe normally and I didn't feel like I had a head in my ribs anymore. I also didn't hear anything, and they didn't lay my baby on my chest like they do in the movies when people have C-sections.

I heard alarms going off and what sounded like people running. I asked my anesthesiologist what was happening. Nobody was talking to me. I kept asking if I could see my baby, and nobody would answer me. My anesthesiologist told me everything was going to be ok and that he was going to get a towel to wipe my face. He came back and laid a cold rag on my forehead, and within a few seconds, I started feeling calm. I asked if he gave me something.

He said, "Yes, just something to help keep you comfortable." I could feel my mom holding my hand. I started crying because I just wanted my baby and nobody was telling me anything. Finally, a nurse came over to my mom. I was trying to hear what she was saying but it was hard with all the alarms and people just yelling different things I didn't understand. I heard her say the baby was not responding and that they were doing everything they could. There was a team en route to help us. I could remember just wanting to get up and get my baby. He just needed me. I physically couldn't move. The anesthesiologist kept telling me everything was going to be ok.

My mom asked the nurse if I could see the baby. She said, "Not right now," and my mom then asked if she could see my baby. The nurse told her, yes, she could look at my baby but not hold my baby. My mom walked over and tried talking to my baby. I heard everyone start yelling that he was peeing. You could feel the relief throughout the room. They needed to move me into a recovery area, and on the way out, they let me touch the top of my baby's head. I just prayed. I needed God to please save my baby. The baby I was never supposed to be able to carry, the baby I could not understand why I was having. All that just went away, and all I wanted was to hold my baby.

As I got moved into a different area, I passed the team coming to get my baby. I don't think I've ever cried so hard or so much for so long. It was time to go back to my room where my kids and step dad were waiting. Waiting for me and my baby. I had no idea how I was going to tell them why I didn't have my baby. My kids were sitting at the window and my stepdad was at the table, all looking but not talking. I believe it was my kids who asked where the baby was. I tried to find the words to explain while trying to get myself to stop crying long enough to explain. I don't think any of us knew what to say. The doctor came in and told us they had my baby stable enough to move, so they were going to Fort Wayne. The doctor said I could see my baby, but there were a lot of wires and machines, so holding my baby was not an option, just touching.

They brought my baby in and inside this clear, machine thing lay the most handsome, dark-haired little boy I had ever seen. He had the chunkiest cheeks and rolls all over. I just held his little hand, continuing to pray while also letting my baby know how much I loved him and how proud I was because he had been a strong, little fighter. I told him he was going to be ok. The doctor said the next 24 hours would be critical but they would call and give me updates as much as they could. I was unable to go to the same hospital because I just had a C-section and I couldn't leave for around 72 hours. My family just held me while we all cried. My step dad talked first, telling me he would be fine and that he and my mom would take turns being with me and my baby. They would also look over my older kids until I got to come home. I Facetimed my daddy and told him the news. He assured me he would be fine, and he couldn't wait to meet his grandbaby.

It was the longest 24 hours of my life. I finally got the call that my baby made it through the critical time, and now it was just going to go day by day. My time was up. I got ready to go to my baby. I just couldn't wait to hold my precious baby. My mom came in and we got ready to go. She looked at me and said, "I know you want to get to your baby but I think you need to go see your daddy." I was confused. I had just talked with him, and he was fine. My mom said it all happened fast but now he was in the hospital and not to be scared if he did not know who I was. I walked into my daddy's room and he was looking out the window.

I said, "Hey Daddy." He rolled his head over to look at me, saying hello. I couldn't tell if he knew it was me. I walked over and sat on his bed. He said, " I want to go home."

I said, "Ok Daddy. I'll go tell your nurse," not realizing that was not the home he wanted to go to. I went back to his room. I sat on his bed, and I asked him if he wanted to see pictures of Remington. He looked up at me, eyes so big, placing his hand on my cheek and saying, "I know Remington."

"You do Daddy?"

"Yes, Remington is your son."

"Yes Daddy, he is." My daddy responded with a "Yeah." My daddy was released home on hospice, not talking or having the strength to feed himself or stay awake. I needed my daddy to see my baby. I knew how much he was looking forward to meeting him. I Facetimed my mom and asked to speak to my daddy as I was going to show him my baby. She reminded me that he was sleeping and he might not wake up. She brought him the iPad and told him it was me and that I was with the baby.

I saw my daddy and I told him, "It's me. Look, here's my baby. It's Remington, Daddy."

My daddy opened his eyes and lifted his arm to point to the screen. He said, "That's my baby, that's my baby." I was shocked as it was the most movement and talking my daddy had done since returning home. I told him, "Yes, this is your baby, Daddy."

Other than mumbles, that would be the last thing I heard my daddy say. It was approximately three days later that my daddy passed away. His funeral was going to be in another state. How was I going to make that happen? My baby was still in the NICU. I met with Remi's team and came up with a care plan while I went to my daddy's funeral. I was leaving Sunday morning. As I woke up to get on the road, Remi's doctor called and said, "Come get your baby through the night." He showed signs he was strong enough and would be able to go home. At that moment, I knew that my daddy was already making moves.

In 2022, I married my husband. I finally found the man of my dreams.

He loved me and my kids. At last, it was my turn to have the happiest ever after…or was it? Not long after I moved to a different state, sold my house along with everything I owned to be with my prince charming and begin our happy life together, I found out my husband had been cheating on me the whole time we had been together, even having his girlfriend at our wedding. I was devastated. My whole world just came crashing down. I had no clue what I was going to do; I knew no one, I didn't have a job, I didn't have a vehicle, nor did I have my own house to go back to. I think the worst part about all of this was that I trusted him so much that I was willing to start over, so I sold everything.

Then, for the first time in a long time, I felt hopeless and defeated. How could this happen? He knew my fears. He knew I suffered from PTSD. It was like none of that mattered - he only cared about himself. I reached out to the other lady's husband, but much to my surprise, my loving husband had already had a conversation with them and told them I was crazy and just jealous that he was friends with their wife. So, the truth of that situation fell on deaf ears. During this time, I learned my whole wedding was a joke, and I was the brunt of it.

I saw messages from his friends telling him that there were better gems out there, and I only married him because I needed a baby daddy and sugar daddy. I laughed reading that this was coming from a person who made fun of me because I liked chicken over steak. It just reminded me that no matter how old someone is, it doesn't mean they are not still childish. I continued reading the judgmental messages along with others coming to me and telling me the things that were said the night before my wedding and during my wedding. I remember I kept asking why. *Why did you do this to me and my kids? Why did you allow people to think and say things about me that are not true? Why did you have your girlfriend at my wedding? Why won't you tell your friends and family the truth about what you did?*

I don't think I'll ever get honest answers to any of those questions. The one thing I do know for sure is that if any of those people would have taken just 10 minutes of their time, then they would know I accomplished more as a single mother than those judgmental bitches ever would accomplish while being married. As I tried to start to pick up the pieces and figure out what my next move would be, I never would've dreamed that fate had yet another twist in store—a work injury that halted my career in its tracks. I was broken. There was no fight left in me at this point.

For the past 17 years, I did it all. I bought and owned my own home. I bought and owned two different Volkswagens. I worked full-time while going through the reserve police academy and raised my kids. I worked 12-16 hour days to provide for my kids, and I walked away from it all with nothing, except my kids of course, to start my dream life with this amazing man, only to find out it all was a lie. Now, I couldn't work to even try to get things back in place for me and my kids. How could I be so damn dumb to trust him like I did? How could I put my kids in a situation like this? I should've known better.

It took me hitting the bottom and having what looked like no way out to realize he might have wanted me, but he sure as hell didn't deserve me. My husband has since been putting in the time and effort to show me he does deserve me, and that he truly does love me and my kids. The journey has not been easy, and I have had to give a lot of grace but every day my husband shows me he's worth the grace.

It was then, in the stillness of recovery, that I heard my true calling. I took an online course and became a certified life coach. My hope is that those who are suffering from depression or struggling with PTSD won't feel alone and will reach out because they want to step back into their empowerment and start living a happier, healthier life. So, with a newfound purpose, I opened Empowerment Journey—a sanctuary for those seeking to reclaim their power and rewrite their stories like so many have had to do. Maybe they too can be the hope others are looking for. Then they could guide others on their journey in stepping back into their empowerment too.

My past may be marked by shadows, but today I stand in the sunshine, guiding others along their path to healing and empowerment. All this while also knowing if not for God, my journey would have looked very different.

Raeyan Goff

EmpowerHer Transitions
Mental Health Coach

www.instagram.com/empowerhertransitions
stan.store/empowerhertransitions

Hello everyone, my name is Rae and I am the CEO of EmpowerHer Transitions, a mental health and mindset coaching brand. You can find us on instagram @empowerhertransitions and book a free coaching call with us. Although I only recently became a mother, I have always been a mompreneur at heart and dedicate myself to helping other mompreneurs. I started my first business in 2019 while still in college and I made $5,000 within 6 months. That sparked the little hustler in me, and now I empower other mothers to start their own businesses. I helped my aunt start and scale her business to 6-figures within the first 2 years. My purpose is to empower young adults, especially mothers, to embrace their struggles freely and with confidence, by knowing that they are not alone. If I can do it at only 25, so can you.

WHEN THE GOING GETS TOUGH, GIVE UP

By Raeyan Goff

Being a new mom at 25 was a dream come true. Growing up, I had always wanted to have my first kid by 25, and after graduating college with my bachelor's in 2021, I felt that there was no better time. However, it wasn't until I graduated with my master's a year later that the dream actually became a reality. And thus, the start of my journey as a mompreneur began. Well, sorta.

As I said, motherhood had always been my dream, so when I had Zion, I already knew that I wanted to start a business to create generational wealth. While I was pregnant, I started a new business, Road to Zion Wellness. I rented an office space with the intention of starting a coaching business to help women achieve self-actualization. Having him born as a preemie only changed that direction a little bit. I went through severe postpartum mental health struggles really bad for the first three months of my son's life which he spent in the NICU. I felt unsupported and like no one understood me, and that was when I realized that I had to do something. *There's got to be other moms out there like me. Young, alone, and scared with no one to turn to,* I thought to myself. I'm a therapist at a nonprofit by day, and I know how to coach myself back to mental sanity, but not everyone does. I wanted Road to Zion Wellness to specifically cater to black preemie mothers, or so I thought.

My entrepreneurial journey has been an interesting one, starting with my first business while still in college as sort of a side hustle. It was a business called HeavenSent RCG, where I sold lip gloss and body care products, mainly to friends, but then it turned into a wholesale business. Within six months of starting it, I had already made $5,000 during the height of the pandemic. This sparked something in me that

I was meant to do more than just work a 9-5. However, when the business got too demanding, I gave up on it to focus on my academics because school always came first. Only, I knew I'd want to start another business again later on. And I had started a few afterward: Luxe Melanin Co, Heaven's Palace, Rae's Essentials.

You see, the problem was never starting the business, that was easy. Staying motivated and continuing is the problem. My brain runs a thousand miles a minute, so I never struggled to come up with business ideas, but I struggled with feeling confident to go when the sales weren't coming in as easily as I'd hoped. So that's what this chapter is going to be about, *when the going gets tough, give up.*

I ended up putting Road to Zion Wellness on hold after my son's 99-day hospital stay, not because I didn't get any sales, but because I never actually started it. I decided that my goal with that business was to turn it into a nonprofit to give back to single mothers, battered women and children, homeless people, and the mentally ill. But as we all know, you need money to start a nonprofit, and lots of it, which brought me to starting Pretty Profit Pioneers and EmpowerHer Transitions, both coaching brands but in different ways.

Pretty Profit Pioneers caters to single or struggling mothers and helps them create generational wealth through passive income. I provide business coaching to startup businesses to help women improve their brand from a four-figure business to a five or six-figure business because I have always had an eye for good business marketing and can point out what businesses are missing. I coached a few women and even helped one create her first passive income by adding another coaching package to her program. Here's her review: "I've done a six-week coaching program with Rae and it has been incredible. She has motivated me and held me accountable to make progress in my business. I've achieved so much in such a short time, thanks so much

Rae." And she's not the only one. I helped my aunt start a scrub business and scale it to a six-figure income within the first three years. And I am even still a business consultant to her every now and then.

So the problem isn't that I don't know how to scale a business, it's just that I'm not motivated enough to stay consistent with my own. I'm a single mother of a premature one-year-old, busy-body little boy, a full-time work-from-home therapist, and a full-time college student at ASU, and I'm working on getting three coaching certifications on top of the confidence coaching certification I already have. I AM BUSY! So with the free time that I do have, I don't like to spend it creating and posting content, engaging with followers, promoting and marketing, and all the behind-the-scenes work. I'm just the brains; I have amazing business ideas, but I need someone else to do the work. Does that mean that I should give up on being a business owner?

NO! It means that I should only be a CEO. According to Northwest Executive Education, "The role of a **CEO (chief executive officer)** is to provide overall direction and leadership for a company. They are responsible for setting the strategic goals and objectives of the organization and ensuring that the necessary resources are in place to achieve them." The CEO makes the decisions about the development of new products and evaluates the efficiency of current products, represents the company, manages the finances, oversees the employees, and creates long-term goals for the company. All of these things (except being the face of the company) are things that I enjoy doing and am great at doing.

There are multiple running parts of a business, and even as a small business owner, you don't have to be expected to do them all. Being overworked and burning out your first year of business is not the goal, especially because we got into our business for a reason. So, I noticed a problem and developed a solution. My therapy clients would always tell me that they struggled with being a mother and also fulfilling their goals and dreams in life, and it made me think, *why don't they feel confident?* And I realized that the problem is simply that society expects too much of us. We have to be an active mom, the chef, the chauffeur, the housekeeper, the tutor, a first friend, the nurse, and sometimes even the breadwinner and still make time to take care of ourselves. To some moms, it all seems impossible. That's because it is.

You do not have to do everything and be everything. As much as I intentionally wanted to be a SUPERMOM, I realized that the only awards you get for that are burnout and a lack of autonomy and self-care. If you don't believe me, read *Year of Yes* by Shonda Rhimes or the multiple short books available on Audible by Rachel Rodgers. Both women are millionaires, fulfilled, and getting the most out of their 24-hour days. How do they do it? The answer is simple - they gave up.

They gave up on doing certain menial tasks so that they could make time for the more important ones. The tasks that would make them more money.

Delegate the tasks that you don't like doing, aren't good at doing, or simply don't have time to do. It's okay to give up on things that you are not good at. If you suck at cleaning up around the house, your kids will not hate you for getting a housekeeper to come around once a week. Or if you burn up the kitchen and can only cook PB&Js and decide to start hiring a chef to do meal prep instead. They might actually appreciate it and love you more for it, especially as a mompreneur. So, the same goes for your business. People created COOs, CFOs, virtual assistants, social media managers, graphic designers, website designers, and so many other business-related positions due to the need.

If done right, and please do your due diligence, delegating your tasks to a virtual assistant or social media manager can not only save you time but also make you millions. Imagine that you invested in a social media manager which frees up time for you to flesh out the million-dollar product that God bestowed upon you. You're able to create a launch plan for it, take the time to create the product, and then send it over to your experienced social media manager who does all the marketing for you, and the money starts rolling in. But what would I know? Except that I've done it myself with my business EmpowerHer Transitions.

EmpowerHer Transitions is a coaching brand that I created to be the business I originally wanted Road to Zion Wellness to be. It's the brand that allows women to feel empowered throughout their hardest and most vulnerable points in life whether health-related, age-related, financial, or mental by empowering women to show up confidently as their truest selves and to live a rich and meaningful life. I do this through individualized growth packages for my clients starting with a minimum of a three-month program for $650 to anywhere up to a year of coaching. I do initial free discovery calls with my clients before delving into mindset and mental health-related coaching sessions after the client signs on. Considering that each coaching package is personally tailored to each client based on their needs assessment (plus there is a lot of research that goes into my coaching sessions for clients), I don't have time to run my Instagram page and create graphics, so I outsourced.

My social media manager posts three to four times a week, creates the graphics, posts on my stories, and does all the engagement while I create the products that reflect my purpose. You see, with Pretty Profit Pioneers, Luxe Melanin Co, Rae's Essentials, and every other brand, I gave up because I didn't want to do the work of social media. And most people made me feel discouraged by telling me, "If you want to be a business owner, you have to do everything yourself, otherwise you're being lazy." But I am here to tell you that's not true. The millionaires aren't doing it, so why do you have to do it all? I believe in working smarter, not harder. Don't get me wrong; not everyone has the financial means to hire a social media manager or a virtual assistant, but that's why you should probably hold off on starting the business until you do. Because bad marketing and lack of consistency of quality content can tarnish a great brand even before it gets started, and I am a testament to that five failed businesses later.

It's not as easy to do social media as it was pre- and peri-pandemic because everyone is doing it now. I don't believe that the market is oversaturated, I just truly believe that you have to invest more time and money into standing out. I was blessed enough to take my own pictures and have my friends promote my lip gloss brand back in 2019 and 2020 with an old iPhone. Taking pictures in my room still gained me almost 700 followers. Now, that doesn't fly. You'll be lucky to even get 100 followers and barely any sales. I recently reached 15,000 accounts in two days with only 40-something followers at the time that my social media manager made two posts. There was nothing inherently special about them except that she knew what she was doing and how to reach my target audience. My business literally blew up because of it with likes, reshares, and comments. Before that, I had never reached more than 50 people on my page and no one was really DMing or commenting.

Believe me, I'm not saying this to discourage you. I'm saying this because it was something that I realized through trial and error. My business is doing so much better now, and yours can too. You don't have to give up on your dreams just because you don't like showing your face or creating content, posting, or responding to emails. You can get somebody else to do it, like that famous TikTok says, and spend your time on something else. As a therapist and coach, I have seen the power that a change in mindset can make for the projection of a person's growth. I believe that everyone can be successful with their businesses as long as they're willing to pass the torch every once in a while. We can all achieve financial success and stability in our lifetime with hard work and dedication, but those who are open-minded and willing to go against the grain simply do it a little bit faster. I'd simply like to end this chapter with this expert from a Yahoo Finance article:

> Self-made millionaire Steve Siebold, who interviewed over 1,200 of the world's wealthiest people before writing "How Rich People Think," echoes this belief.
>
> Rich people have an action mentality and are problem solvers. "While the masses are waiting to pick the right numbers and praying for prosperity, the great ones are solving problems," he writes.
>
> This doesn't mean they're smarter than the average person, as Jobs noted. "They are just more strategic," Siebold explains. "When the rich need money, they don't wonder if it's possible, they simply begin creating new ideas that solve problems."
>
> And "the bigger the problem you solve, the more money you make," he says.
>
> At the end of the day, getting rich is an inside job. "Let's set the record straight once and for all: Anyone can become wealthy," Siebold writes. "It has nothing to do with your education or where you come from. It's not what you do that guarantees wealth, it's what you are."

We were all created with a purpose, and mine is to EmpowerHer Transitions through this life by promoting wholeness and confidence amongst ourselves through coaching, self-development resources such as journals and workbooks, and eventually a solo book, but even more so, it was to be here, at this moment, in our to empower your transition. Follow us on Instagram @empowerhertransitions and click the link in the bio to become more empowered along your journey.

Rebecca Washington

Owner & CEO of Social Media Strategist
Legendary Virtual Solutions

https://www.linkedin.com/in/BexWashington
https://www.facebook.com/wife.mom.legendary
https://instagram.com/wife.mom.legendary
http://www.wifemomlegend.contactin.bio/

Hi I'm Bex. I'm a wife, a mom & owner/CEO of Legendary Virtual Solutions. Consider me your social media bestie! I love helping individuals & companies shine through digital marketing & social media strategy. Every client is given personalized attention & VIP service. I value excellent communication & provide quick turnaround time on assignments. The foundation of my experience & professional development began while working for a Fortune 500 company. I received corporate training & knowledge that has set me up for success in my personal business. I take pride in regularly exceeding my clients' expectations. My friends consider me as the "recovering perfectionist" & problem solver of the group. Attention to detail is second nature to me. Outside of running my business as a "mompreneur" I also homeschool my daughter. I strive to give her an enriched childhood full of education, experiences, travel & memories.

LIFE OF BEX: MOMPRENEUR MASTERY

By Rebecca Washington

Hi, I'm Bex! I'm a wife, a (homeschool) mom, and the owner of Legendary Virtual Solutions. Being a mom entrepreneur is a journey filled with unique challenges and rewards. Add homeschooling to the mix, and the balancing act becomes even more intricate. From managing a household and nurturing relationships to running a business and guiding a child's education, navigating these diverse roles requires a delicate balance and a deep sense of purpose. In this chapter, we'll explore how I've managed to run a successful social media management business while homeschooling my daughter, highlighting the strategies and mindset shifts that have helped me find harmony in the chaos of work and family life. Here is my story.

My very first "job" or "business" as a thirteen-year-old was helping an elderly family friend learn how to use her new computer by giving her private lessons. I guess you could say that is where my love of entrepreneurship began. In my twenties, before becoming a mom, my corporate career was in the hospitality industry for a Fortune 500 company. I received my foundational experience and training while working there. After having my daughter, I knew the corporate world was no longer a great fit for me. I wanted to contribute to the household financially, but I felt like my daughter deserved a super present mom. For many years, I took a step back from my career and raised our daughter while homeschooling her as well. I knew that was the direction we wanted to go for her. I also knew that even though we were making the financial sacrifices necessary, as far as the long-term vision went, we needed a different path. Fast-forward a few years, I had begun helping a few friends who had businesses with their marketing and social media. I have always had such a passion and intrigue for social media and its ever-changing platforms. I've also enjoyed staying up to date and in the know about digital marketing trends. Word of mouth quickly spread and social media and digital marketing were my strong suits. One day, during a very rough patch in my life, I asked myself what I had to lose in starting my own business and pursuing having my very own business. I had seen how many moms were doing virtual assisting and social media management, and I figured why not give it a try? I invested a few days working on my resume, designed a LinkedIn profile, gathered "reviews" from friends I had assisted, and created some visual graphics/info cards. My next step was networking myself, posting on my own social media accounts, joining Facebook groups targeting my ideal clients, and applying to any leads I could find. A few days later, one of my very first clients who had reached out and contacted me happened to be a mega influencer! That was the birth of my entrepreneurship and business.

Fast-forward one year later, and the business has really grown. I put myself out there and worked through some really difficult imposter syndrome. I have had the privilege of helping several large clients. My sweet spot, however, is working with just two at a time. I like to give a very personal and VIP service to my clients and am able to still have the majority of my day to spend with my daughter. I have been asked to speak at homeschooling mom group seminars and conduct Q&As at conferences to help give advice and tips to other moms looking to start their entrepreneurial journeys. Likewise, I have helped many close friends start their path to "mompreneurship." Not only that, but I have been able to take this business across state lines due to a move we made for my husband's career. I have been able to take extended vacations thanks to homeschooling and my business both being virtual and mobile. I think one of the biggest achievements is being able to set a great example for my daughter in going after what she loves and making time for the more important things in life (family time, relationship with God, etc).

Balancing work and homeschooling requires careful planning, flexibility, and time management. I've found that setting clear boundaries and priorities is crucial. Each day, I establish a schedule that includes dedicated work hours and homeschooling blocks. Some days may require a little more homeschool attention and other days may have things pop up from my clients that need to be handled. Sometimes I work early in the day, and other times I work late at night when my daughter is asleep. This helps me stay focused and ensures that both my business and my daughter's education receive the attention they deserve. I highly suggest time blocking or making a schedule that works for you but be prepared to be flexible as well.

What is it that I do specifically as a social media strategist/manager? Well, it involves overseeing and executing a business's or individual's/ influencer's social media strategy. It encompasses a range of tasks aimed at building brand awareness, engaging with the audience, and driving traffic and conversions. Here are some key aspects of social media management:

1. **Strategy Development:** This includes setting goals, identifying target audiences, choosing the right social media platforms, and creating a content calendar.

2. **Content Creation:** Creating and curating content that resonates with the audience, including posts, images, videos, and articles.

3. **Community Engagement:** Responding to comments, messages, and mentions, and actively engaging with the audience to build relationships and foster a sense of community.

4. **Analytics and Reporting:** Monitoring and analyzing social media performance metrics, such as reach, engagement, and conversion rates, and using this data to optimize strategies and campaigns.

5. **Paid Advertising:** Managing paid social media campaigns to reach a larger audience and achieve specific business objectives, such as lead generation or sales.

6. **Influencer Partnerships:** Collaborating with influencers and brand advocates to amplify reach and credibility.

7. **Crisis Management:** Handling negative feedback or crises that may arise on social media in a timely and professional manner.

8. **Stay Updated:** Keeping abreast of the latest trends and best practices in social media marketing to ensure strategies remain effective and competitive.

Overall, social media management is about building and maintaining a strong online presence, fostering engagement with the audience, and driving business growth through social media channels.

So what does a typical day look like for me? My day typically begins early, often before the rest of the household stirs, as I carve out morning rituals such as enjoying a cup of coffee with my dog and cat by my side with the fireplace crackling in the background. I then begin managing social media accounts, crafting strategies for clients, and attending virtual meetings. Homeschooling sessions typically are between 9:30 am and 11:30 am where I transform into a teacher, guiding my daughter through lessons and engaging in educational activities. I strive to bond with her, instilling not just knowledge but also values and life skills. We frequently engage in outings with friends & homeschool field trip days. I also manage the household, tackling chores and errands as they arise. As the day draws to a close, I try to wrap up any loose ends or projects for my clients, send off emails, and focus on plans for the next day, knowing that each day brings new challenges and triumphs.

Having a strong support system is essential for mom entrepreneurs. As a kid with my own business, my parents were very much my biggest supporters. I had no idea what I was capable of until they showed me I was. My husband has been a critical part of this puzzle while trying to do "all the things." Many days if I have a rush situation with a client he is willing to help our daughter with her schoolwork when he gets home. On his days off, he encourages me to take some "me time." He is and has always been one of my biggest cheerleaders when I have had moments of insecurity or doubt. I've found support in online communities of fellow "mompreneurs" and homeschooling parents. These communities provide a space to share experiences, seek advice, and find encouragement during challenging times. I also have very close and dear friends who have chosen similar paths in life. They have been crucial in battling my imposter syndrome and cheering me on when the self-doubt monster rears its ugly head. Lots of late-night conversations, questions, advice, funny memes, and vent sessions that get me through.

Self-care is often neglected when balancing work, homeschooling, and family responsibilities. However, I've learned that taking care of myself is essential for maintaining productivity and well-being. Whether it's through exercise, hobbies, or simply taking a break (aka a nap), prioritizing self-care has been crucial to my success as a mom entrepreneur. I love fun outings, doing personal Bible study, spending time with friends, helping others with their business goals, taking an evening walk in our neighborhood, doing silly TikToks, or just taking a relaxing hot bubble bath with a glass of wine. And I always try to work in a digital detox when possible.

Why do I feel that Social media is important for ANY entrepreneur? There are several reasons:

1. **Visibility and Brand Building:** Social media provides a platform for entrepreneurs to showcase their brands, products, and services to a wide audience. It allows them to establish and

build their brand identity, making it easier for potential customers to recognize and connect with them.

2. **Audience Engagement:** Social media enables entrepreneurs to engage directly with their audience, fostering relationships and building a loyal customer base. It provides a channel for two-way communication, allowing entrepreneurs to gather feedback, address customer concerns, and create a more personalized experience for their audience.

3. **Marketing and Promotion:** Social media is a powerful marketing tool that allows entrepreneurs to reach a large audience with targeted messaging. It provides cost-effective advertising options, allowing entrepreneurs to promote their products or services to specific demographics or interest groups.

4. **Market Research:** Social media provides valuable insights into customer behavior, preferences, and trends. Entrepreneurs can use this information to refine their products or services, develop new offerings, and stay ahead of the competition.

5. **Networking and Partnerships:** Social media provides entrepreneurs with the opportunity to connect with other professionals in their industry, potential collaborators, and industry influencers. This networking can lead to valuable partnerships, collaborations, and business opportunities.

6. **Driving Website Traffic and Sales:** Social media can drive traffic to an entrepreneur's website or online store, increasing visibility and sales. By sharing engaging content and promotions, entrepreneurs can encourage their social media followers to visit their website and make a purchase.

Overall, social media is a valuable tool for entrepreneurs to build their brand, engage with their audience, market their products or services, and stay competitive in today's digital landscape. There is not one company, product, or person who has a business that will not benefit from a strong social media presence. No matter what direction your entrepreneurship takes you, please remember to invest in marketing yourself! You have remarkable skills and ideas others need to know about! Your business will undoubtedly grow by utilizing social media and marketing specifically catered toward your goals. Put yourself out there - you have nothing to lose.

What are some of my tips on marketing yourself? Marketing oneself as an entrepreneur requires a strategic approach that highlights one's unique skills, experiences, and value proposition.

First and foremost, it's essential to **clearly define your target audience** and understand their needs and preferences. This knowledge will guide your marketing efforts and help you tailor your message to resonate with potential clients or customers.

Building a **strong personal brand** is key to standing out in a competitive market. This involves creating a compelling narrative that showcases your expertise, passion, and credibility. Utilize social media platforms, blogs, and professional networking sites to share valuable content, engage with your audience, and establish yourself as a thought leader in your industry.

Networking is another crucial aspect of marketing oneself as an entrepreneur. Attend industry events, conferences, and networking groups to connect with like-minded professionals and expand your reach. Building relationships and fostering partnerships can open doors to new opportunities and collaborations.

Consistency is key when it comes to marketing yourself. Maintain a consistent brand voice and visual identity across all channels to reinforce your message and build brand recognition. By effectively marketing yourself as an entrepreneur, you can attract clients, investors, and collaborators who align with your vision and contribute to your success.

Balancing mompreneurship, homeschooling, and business growth is no easy feat, but with the right strategies and mindset, it's possible to find success. By prioritizing time management, creating a support system, maintaining self-care, and focusing on business growth, I've been able to create a fulfilling and harmonious life that works for me and my family. I am confident you can do the same!

One of my favorite quotes is "Life begins at the end of your comfort zone," as said by Neale Donald Walsch. Keeping your "reason why" at the forefront of your vision will always be helpful. I knew the kind of life I wanted for my daughter and had to remind myself of that daily. She was the reason I was having sleepless nights, anxiety, and worrisome moments. She was also the reason I was able to homeschool and give her life experiences and plenty of travel memories. Furthermore, she was most definitely the reason I pushed myself so I could bring home a full-time income, working only a few hours a day if that!

To all those in my life who have supported me, thank you! To my daughter Kaia, I love you, and I hope when you're older you'll look back on your childhood and be proud of me. For those of you reading this, I wish you nothing but the best. I am excited about what your future holds! I hope my thoughts have been encouraging and helpful. Moreover, I would love to hear from you and connect! You can find me on all socials @Wife.Mom.Legendary

Samantha Sheppard

Founder & CEO of Samantha Sheppard Consulting

https://www.linkedin.com/in/samanthaksheppard/
https://www.facebook.com/groups/marketingmadeeasywithsamantha
https://www.instagram.com/ssheppard.consulting/
www.samanthasheppardconsulting.com
https://linktr.ee/sheppardconsulting

I am from PA and the owner and founder of Samantha Sheppard Consulting.

With a degree in marketing and over 20 years experience in the field, I am focused on helping other women in business reach their goals through teaching easy + proven successful marketing strategies. I do this by providing a variety of courses and consultation services that will allow you to stand up and stand out in today's noisy world. Whether you're just getting started OR you are a seasoned entrepreneur looking for some fresh and new ideas, I am here to help!

TWO STEPS FORWARD + ONE STEP BACK IS STILL PROGRESS!

By Samantha Sheppard

As a mother and entrepreneur, I've faced the balancing act of family and business, striving for perfection while juggling it all. In the modern world of womanhood, the threads of motherhood and entrepreneurship are deeply woven together, creating a wonderful yet often overwhelming collage of roles, responsibilities, and aspirations. As a mother and entrepreneur myself, I have navigated through all of the expectations set before me and struggled with the elusive pursuit of perfection while focusing on nurturing my family, growing my business, and maintaining my sanity amidst the chaos.

It's a journey marked by two steps forward, and one step back – a dance of progress and happy dances while also being paralleled by setbacks and frustrations that embody the essence of the woman experience. This chapter dives into the ups and downs of this journey, emphasizing the importance of progress over perfection and the need for boundaries. Join me as we explore the challenges, victories, and lessons learned along the way, shaping a journey of growth, resilience, and empowerment.

As a mom, I feel that sometimes my life is two steps forward and one step back. Still moving in the right direction but frustrated that I can't just keep moving forward without the backstepping.

That's just not reality. Especially for a mompreneur with two teenage daughters, a home to run, and a business to build, getting over the idea that every day would be simply perfect was a harsh reality for me.

To be honest with you, when my girls were little, I remember vividly crying in my living room feeling like I was failing at motherhood and entrepreneurship. That wasn't actually what was happening, but it was my reality. I wanted to show up 100% for my girls, my husband, my friends, my clients, and my community around me, but it was in that moment of breakdown that I realized I had to get over my vision of perfection that I, for some reason, put upon myself.

Nobody else told me I had to be perfect. It was all my fault. I had it in my mind that in order for me to be "successful", I had to be there for everybody all the time. Which meant always showing up for others and never saying the dreaded word 'no'. The only reality that this creates is one that is filled with frustration and exhaustion, with moments of joy sprinkled in between.

Why do we, as women, put these unrealistic expectations on ourselves and set ourselves up for failure? I know I can't be the only one who has been through this. I have no idea where that concept came from, but the more women I speak to, I realize that this is an unattainable goal we put in our brains and then kill ourselves every day trying to live up to it.

Well, I'm here to tell you in the most loving way that we need to get over it. The goal should be progress over perfection. That's it. Two Steps Forward, One Step Back. If we are still moving forward, growing, learning, and succeeding.... we need to take that ridiculous idea of perfection and throw it out the window as far as we can.

We need to set ourselves up for success, not stress. We need to set ourselves up for a life full of peace, joy, happiness, and love. But here is the million-dollar question - where do we start? Well, one way is to start by looking in the mirror and telling ourselves that it's OK to not be perfect. (sometimes easier said than done). There is not one human being on the earth that fits that description of perfection.

This unrealistic viewpoint can be shifted to create a healthier version of reality for our lives that allows us to truly have peace in all aspects of our lives without trying to kill ourselves trying to be perfect. I have come to this realization: it is all about *boundaries*. We must put in place healthy boundaries for our work life, family life, and our responsibilities. These boundaries must reflect the values that stand strong in our lives and ones that will allow us to flourish and succeed, not stress and fail.

When I realized that implementing boundaries was a great place for me to start living a life with less stress and more progress, I began with step one - saying NO to different people and things in my life. When I began implementing these boundaries, I found out something shocking. The only people who had a problem with me setting these limitations were the ones who were abusing the fact that I never said no. That was a huge eye-opener for me to see who in my life was taking advantage of me and who supported this new outlook.

Does the thought of saying 'no' create immediate stress for you? Or maybe it already gives you a false sense of failure? Acknowledging our gut reactions is the first step to change. Change is not always comfortable and it usually creates uneasiness at first…. but change does not need to be a bad thing! If you constantly remind yourself of why you are going to implement boundaries, it makes the transition easier.

After embracing the fact that boundaries were needed, then came the fear of worrying about disappointing others. This was a hard reality for me, even though it was mostly in my own head because I truly did want to be the person that others could count on and ask for help. However, I was sick and tired of always feeling sick and tired. I was constantly mentally and physically exhausted. So what helped me with this next step in the shift to implementing boundaries? I realized that if I had healthy boundaries, it would allow me to show up BETTER in every area of my life. I discovered that I had to stop renting away my time (and sanity) to make others happy. It was not only hurting myself but also my family and my business.

We will be the only guardians of our own peace. Others will not do this for us and for that reason, we have to take personal responsibility for putting limitations and boundaries on what gets our time and attention. This will enable us to be more productive and successful in all areas of our lives.

Creating those boundaries in your life, both mentally and physically, is critically important for embracing a life of progress over perfection. It took me a long time to develop healthy boundaries and it almost killed me for the lack of them. You see, my husband and I have been entrepreneurs for 20 years and have gone through every stage of life and adulthood in the world of business ownership. When we started our family, that's when I look back and truly see where that unrealistic expectation of perfection blossomed in my brain.

I was trying to be the PTO preschool mom, the successful business owner, the best wife, and the best mother that I could be… and it was killing me. I had the best of intentions but I was blinded by my own unrealistic ideas of what I 'should' be doing in order to meet my definition of what a successful woman is. If I'm honest with myself, I can barely count the number of times I said "no" when I was asked to do something. I wanted to do all of those things. I wanted to be there for everyone. I wanted to show up and be the person that others could count on. However, when that compounded out year over year and I kept ignoring the signs that my body was trying to tell me that something was wrong, that's when it came to a point where I didn't have a choice and I HAD to say no and make a change. It was in those days that I quickly realized that I had to make a huge shift in my life: I had to say 'no' to others so I would not have to say 'no' to my family and myself.

You see, I had given so much of my time and attention to others that I completely ignored what my body was trying to tell me. If I'm honest, I had not paid attention to my health for years and it got to the point where I couldn't get off the couch, I couldn't take care of my children and I couldn't show up at all for my business. I eventually found out that I had Lyme disease so severe that it was shutting down my organs and killing me from the inside out. After getting diagnosed, my family and I had to move to Arizona for several months to undergo treatment that saved my life.

During treatment, I literally couldn't do anything except sit in a treatment chair for eight hours a day. I had a lot of time for personal reflection. I realized that by trying to live up to this unrealistic ideal of perfection, I ran the risk of not being there for my family and those I love. In those moments, I embraced that I had to create healthy boundaries (and actually stick to them) if I wanted to survive and thrive.

Fast forward to today - I still cringe every time I have to say "no" but I know it's in the best interest of myself, my family, and my business. Ladies, it's impossible to be everywhere all the time for everybody… impossible! We as women are incredible beings but we are not superpowered with unlimited amounts of strength, endurance, and time. We have to work within the boundaries of our lives in order to show up as our BEST selves.

Two steps forward one step back is living out the pursuit of a life of progress over perfection. It's embracing the fact that we have been given gifts and talents that the world needs to know about. However, if we kill ourselves in the process, what kind of person will we be?

I pray that you never have to get to the point where I did before setting healthy boundaries, and that is why I wanted to write this chapter. To share my story with you and give you a glimpse into what can happen if we don't have healthy boundaries. You CAN stand up and stand out in this world by creating healthy boundaries and still succeed. Give yourself grace and space so you can flourish to levels you can't even imagine!

My encouragement to you is this: take a few minutes to really sit down and reflect on your life. Look at the choices that you make every day and decide if they bring you joy. Stress? Frustration? And I encourage you to even talk to somebody trusted in your life to help you establish those healthy boundaries because sometimes we are so blinded by our own ambition that we can't even see what is hurting us.

You have so much to offer the world, just remember progress over perfection! I am cheering for you!

Sara Ross

Business Coach

www.facebook.com/thesaraross
www.instagram.com/thesaraross
www.thesaraross.com

Sara Ross, a Business Coach for Moms, specializes in visibility and collaborations through strategic partnerships. With a focus on leveraging the power of summits and bundles, she guides mom entrepreneurs to boost their visibility and increase sales. Offering personalized guidance and support, Sara equips her clients to stand out in competitive markets and achieve their entrepreneurial goals. Driven by her passion for assisting fellow mom entrepreneurs in achieving success and leaving a lasting legacy for their family. Sara resides in Missouri with her husband and four children. Her favorite season is summer, where she loves the opportunity to have her kids home and spend quality time together by the pool. Obsessed with thrift store hauls and full-time RV adventures on YouTube, Sara envisions creating unforgettable memories traveling the United States full-time in her own RV with her loved ones.

BEYOND LIMITS: RISING ABOVE LIFE'S CHALLENGES TO BUILD YOUR BUSINESS LEGACY

By Sara Ross

I. Introduction

I never imagined how tough this journey into entrepreneurship would be. You know, when you Google it, they say around 90% of startups fail, and most of them fail within years two and five. Now, if I had to guess, some of those failures come down to not having the right skills or knack for running a business.

But honestly, I think a big part of these failures is due to life throwing curveballs at you left and right. I mean, life is like a roller coaster full of ups and downs, especially for us moms. We are constantly juggling a million things at once, and when life gets hard, some things gotta go. Unfortunately, too often, it's our dreams that get shoved on the back burner.

I've faced my fair share of life's hurdles and business setbacks. Through it all, I've come to realize that challenges are simply part of the journey, and it's OK to prioritize my dreams. I've learned that overcoming obstacles is within me and that striving to create a lasting legacy of entrepreneurship is not just for me but for my family too. This business venture isn't just about fulfilling my own aspirations; it's about building a brighter future for those I love most.

II. Embracing Challenges

In 2017, my entrepreneurial adventure began when I discovered a network marketing company. I was already loving their products, so when they presented the business opportunity, I was all in! It seemed like a no-brainer decision.

If you've ever been part of a network marketing company you probably either loved it or hated it. Honestly, when I first got into it, I had no idea there was so much negativity around network marketing and direct selling.

But as I started putting their methods into practice, I began to get why some weren't big fans. I knew there had to be a better way to grow a business than bombarding everyone I had ever met in my life with cold messages.

So, I made it my mission to figure out a new, more genuine way to make it work. Because, let's face it, nobody wants to be that person filling up their friends' inboxes with sales pitches.

My solution: Instagram.

It was back when Instagram was full of picture-perfect feeds filled with flat lays and curated images. I jumped in with both feet, plastering my network marketing products all over my feed. I even dabbled in blogging and Pinterest, hoping to give my business a boost. But despite all my efforts, my business just couldn't seem to take off.

Eventually, I realized I loved the design aspects of online marketing, and I fell in love with using Canva. In 2019, I started selling lead magnets and Pinterest designs on Fiverr as a way to hold my business over until I could finally get my network marketing business off the ground.

On March 21, 2020, my youngest was born. He came into the world just as everything around us was spiraling into uncertainty. Cities and states were already shutting down, and we were all holding our breaths to see what would happen.

I will never forget coming home from the hospital to a world that seemingly pressed pause – no one was going back to school or work, and we were officially on lockdown.

That period was beyond challenging. There I was with a newborn, a four-year-old, a seven-year-old, a 13-year-old, and a husband all at home, trying to juggle this new normal of working and schooling from home. I know I don't have to remind you of the rollercoaster of emotions that time was.

It took me a good six months to even begin to feel like myself again. During that time, I had to put a pause on selling on Fiverr. My mental capacity was stretched to its limit, and I just couldn't juggle everything

However, the entrepreneurial bug never left. I was still dead set on growing my network marketing business without resorting to cold messaging. So, in October 2020, I did what any entrepreneur would - I enrolled in a $3000 Facebook Ads program.

I was convinced it would be the game-changer I needed, allowing me to connect with people who were genuinely interested in what I had to offer without the need for any cold outreach.

Can you guess what happened? Yep, I spent a lot of money trying to bring business builders into my network marketing business without a single one actually joining.

I was at a point in my entrepreneurial journey where I had hit a wall. I was stuck, unsure of how to break through, and the thought of giving up lingered in the back of my mind. But deep down, I knew that wasn't an option. It was a make-it-or-break-it moment, and in times like those, what do you do?

You do what every broke and desperate entrepreneur does.

You hesitantly join another program that once again promises the moon and stars, praying that this time it's different.

In March of 2021, I went into the program with the same, unwavering determination and direction. I was dead set on making this network marketing gig work.

The whole concept of this program was to grow my leads and sales by borrowing other people's audiences using a virtual summit, but before we got the summit, I dived deep into my target market, creating an offer, developing a lead magnet, a masterclass, and a challenge.

I won't lie, when I first started I was a little all over the place. I was juggling both the product and business sides of my network marketing business. It wasn't the smoothest ride, and it led to stalled progress and a feeling of not excelling in either aspect.

I settled on business builders, yet again, because at the end of the day, I LOVED the business side and could talk about that all day long.

When it came time to plan the summit, I knew I needed ample time. Typically, a summit requires about a 90-day lead time, but given this was my first time and the holidays were coming up (it was nearing the end of October), I decided to double the timeline.

With a date firmly set in my mind, I began weaving together my ideas and plans. April 2022 was going to mark the debut of my very first summit and let me tell you I was brimming with excitement.

Little did I know my world was about to be turned upside down.

We're fortunate to live close to my husband's family, where he is one of four brothers, and we've all built a strong bond, forming a close-knit circle. No sooner did I set my date than we received news that deeply impacted our family. It was a challenging time when our once-strong bonds were broken.

I found myself caught in the middle of a falling out and tensions between loved ones, struggling to navigate this new normal. Despite my best efforts to help, I was overwhelmed by the weight of the situation. I began experiencing severe anxiety and debilitating panic attacks.

I wish I could say I sought help from a doctor right away, but the truth is, it took me about five months before I reached my breaking point. I couldn't bear another moment of enduring panic attacks, sacrificing my business, or allowing someone else's actions to dictate my life. What had happened to me was entirely beyond my control, yet I was letting it consume me and derail my dreams and passions. Enough was enough.

The first thing I tackled was my business. I figured if I could just get my schedule in order, I could dive back into building my business with full force. So, what did I do? You guessed it – I sought out an expert in productivity for moms and dove right in.

Around the same time, I also finally made the decision to see a doctor and was prescribed anxiety medication. It was a pivotal moment for me, taking concrete steps towards reclaiming control over my life and well-being.

I reached a point where I wasn't experiencing any panic attacks, and my business was back on track. With newfound clarity and determination, I set a new date for my summit: October 2022. It felt like a fresh start, a chance to pursue my goals with renewed vigor and a solid foundation to build upon.

And you know what happened?

I hosted MY FIRST SUMMIT!! And let me tell you, it was nothing short of amazing. As someone who's typically an introvert, overcoming panic attacks to achieve this milestone felt incredibly empowering. I savored every minute of the experience.

For the first time ever, I felt like I was truly moving my business forward. It was a moment of triumph, a testament to my resilience and determination to turn adversity into opportunity.

Before I take you farther on the journey, I should probably backtrack for a moment. My initial plan with the summit was to grow my network marketing business. However, about a month before the launch, I underwent a complete pivot.

Through my journey, I gained valuable insights and a deeper understanding of why my network marketing business never took off. It became clear to me that did have the knowledge and expertise needed to guide other mom entrepreneurs. I was showing them how to start and grow their online business without all the costly mistakes I had made.

With this newfound clarity, I made the decision to launch my new business as a business coach for moms.

Through my journey, I gained valuable insights and a deep understanding of why my network marketing business had faltered. It became clear to me that I possessed the knowledge and expertise to guide other brand-new business owners, steering them away from the costly mistakes I had made. I saw an opportunity to help them kickstart their ventures in the right direction.

So, with a newfound clarity on my purpose and business goals, I made the bold decision to launch as a business coach.

In 2023, my business kept moving forward, and I started to see my hard work pay off. It was slow but it was good. I had gone from running a business very sporadically to committing to something full time, or at least as full time as I could be while still being a stay-at-home mom.

I set out to host my second summit, the time in September 2023. I started the planning phase in May and conducted interviews throughout the summer months. It was so nice to be able to stay home with my kids, enjoying the summer break, while still making strides in my business.

For the first time in a long time, I felt like I was in a genuinely good place both personally and professionally. It was a reassuring feeling, knowing I was on the right path and making a meaningful impact.

Summit planning was going well. At this time, my house had become the summer hangout, and I had three extra teens practically living with us. I remember one day in particular, July 17th, a day that started off seemingly normal with me drilling it into the kids that I needed complete silence (no yelling, no loud music, etc.) for a summit interview.

Thankfully, my summit interview went off without a hitch. But my day was about to change.

Out of nowhere, I heard a loud bang. My initial thought was that one of the teens had accidentally caused some sort of mini-explosion with a vape device (though I wasn't sure if that was even possible).

Rushing out of my room, I was confronted with a scene far more terrifying than I could have imagined. One of my son's friends was standing at the top of the basement stairs, bleeding, and it slowly dawned on me that the loud bang I had heard was actually a gunshot.

Instinctively, I rushed to protect my three little ones by locking them in my bathroom. With trembling hands, I dialed 911, but before I could speak, one of the older kids managed to get through first. My oldest son and four of his friends were in the basement at the time, and everything seemed to unfold slowly and rapidly all at once.

The sound of sirens filled the air as the police arrived first followed by the ambulance. I did my best to recount what had happened to the officers as they began their search for the gun which was now missing.

None of the kids were talking. The cops combed through my basement, but the gun was nowhere to be found. Four hours passed as the search continued. Eventually, there was a confession, and it was revealed that the gun had been hidden outside and tossed into a sewer drain. Somehow, before I had made it downstairs, one of the kids was able to make it outside to the backyard to toss the gun.

It was a moment of relief mixed with disbelief at what just happened in my home. Once again, my world was turned upside down in an instant. Again, by choices out of my control.

The friend who was shot had actually shot himself, but miraculously, he made a full recovery. It's difficult to describe what happened that day and how things could have turned out drastically different. I thank God for surrounding our house that day.

The days following were extremely hard. I had a family I was trying to hold together, and I was in the midst of planning a summit at the same time. I couldn't put my business on the back burner like I had in the past.

My lesson about not allowing other people's choices to derail my dreams came full circle. And I'm proud to say that I didn't let it stop me. Yes, I took a week off to process everything, but then I got right back into the swing of things the following week. Granted, it was summertime, so I wasn't hustling or working non-stop. I took a breather, gathered my strength, and took each day as it came.

The summit successfully launched in September 2023, and by December of the same year, I even hosted a bundle. My dreams never stopped, and neither did my business.

Fast forward to today, as I write this, I'm in the midst of planning my fourth event and my third summit for April 2024. My business is steadily moving in the right direction, and my word for the year is "resilience." It's a testament to the strength and determination that lies within me despite the challenges and setbacks I've faced along the way.

III. Cultivating Resilience

You might be thinking, "OMG, I can't even imagine going through that," or perhaps you're considering your own struggles and thinking they pale in comparison. But here's the thing: we all have our own stories, our own battles to fight. It doesn't matter what your "hard" is; what matters is resilience. It's the key to navigating through life's challenges, no matter how daunting they may seem.

According to the Cambridge Dictionary, resilience is defined as "the ability to be happy, successful, etc. again after something difficult or bad has happened."

I've faced some incredibly dark times in my life. Mentally I wasn't in a good place, and I had to dig myself out of a hole that seemed impossible to surmount. Even now, I still struggle. It will probably be something I will struggle with my whole life.

Yet, despite the darkness, I believe I'm here for a purpose. I have four kiddos, a loving husband, a thriving business, and my own dreams and aspirations to live for. These are the things that give me strength and motivation to keep pushing forward, to find happiness and success again, no matter how difficult the journey may be.

Here are a few things that help me when I feel like I can't take another step forward:

1. **Pause and breathe.** Take a moment to think of something you're grateful for, no matter how small. It could be as simple as the fact that you woke up this morning and are breathing. On really tough days, you might need to do this every hour or more.

2. **Keep things as simple as possible.** Life can be incredibly complicated, sometimes without any clear reason. Try to simplify your schedules, systems, and your home as much as

you can. Even though things can still feel overwhelming at times, it's much easier to regain your footing when you start from a place of simplicity.

3. **Find something for yourself.** It could be something small, like putting on a face mask every Sunday evening for a bit of self-care, going for a walk outside, or enjoying lunch in the sunshine. Alternatively, it could be something bigger, like taking a solo weekend trip, treating yourself to a spa day, or having lunch out with friends. Whatever it is, make sure it brings you joy and rejuvenates your soul.

4. **Your mindset is crucial.** While this probably should have been number one, I cannot stress enough how much your mindset can impact your experience. When things feel bleak, it's natural to become more cynical, and negative thoughts may swirl around in your head. However, what you think will ultimately influence how you feel. Cultivating a positive mindset, even in the face of adversity, can make a world of difference in how you navigate through challenges and find resilience.

IV. Turning Setbacks into Success

As you have read from my story, other stories, and your own life experiences, setbacks are an inevitable part of the journey. But it doesn't mean you can't be successful. They're simply stepping stones along the path to growth and achievement.

Looking back at my own entrepreneurial journey over the last seven years, there have been countless moments where I could have thrown in the towel. Yet, with every step of my journey, I was able to take those setbacks and turn them into success. Perhaps not always in terms of monetary value, but certainly in terms of strength, knowledge, and personal growth.

Each phase of my business happened for a reason and has led me to where I am today. I often wonder what would have happened if I had achieved massive success within my network marketing business using marketing strategies that didn't feel aligned with me. Would I have been truly happy? Would I have felt fulfilled teaching others to grow their businesses in the same way?

I also reflect on the beginning of my coaching career and my initial goal of bringing on 20+ clients. Would I have been equipped to handle that many people and deliver the results I had promised?

Even when things didn't unfold as I had originally planned, there was always a lesson to be learned. And every single setback has ultimately led me to this moment in time.

Setbacks can always be turned into successes. Consider your own business journey. What lessons are you learning, and how can you leverage them to propel yourself forward? How can you use these setbacks as fuel to keep moving towards your goals? It's all part of the journey, and with the right mindset, every setback becomes an opportunity for growth and success.

V. Building Your Business Legacy

Something I often hear from mom entrepreneurs is that they're either looking to replace a full-time income or seeking something to call their own outside of motherhood. No matter which one you resonate more with, it's common to wonder if pursuing your business dreams is worth it, especially when faced with challenges or financial struggles in the beginning.

Let me assure you that wanting to pursue your dreams is not selfish. While it's true that our children are our main priority, building a business is about more than just ourselves. It's about creating a legacy for our children and future generations.

Part of the legacy I'm building is showing my kids that hard work does pay off, but it's also important not to overwork and live solely for work. I want to instill in them the idea that there are alternative ways to earn a living beyond the typical 9-5 grind. I want to nurture in them a love for travel and experiences, knowing that my business contributes to making those adventures possible.

Like myself, I am sure you know the legacy you want to build for your kids. If you haven't put much thought into it, I encourage you to think about your values, passions, and long-term goals for your business. Consider how you can build a meaningful legacy through your business.

Your kids are watching you. What do you want them to see?

VI. Empowering Others

It is important to not only get your family involved in your business but to surround yourself with a community. If you are working from home, especially online, it can seem like a very lonely place. However, if you're feeling that way, rest assured that there are other mom entrepreneurs who can relate.

There's something truly special about connecting with someone who shares your excitement about launching a new landing page or creating an opt-in to share with the world. Not everyone is going to know what that even means, but within your community of mom entrepreneurs, you'll find your people who get it.

Building your community of mom entrepreneurs can be a lifeline during tough times—it's another valuable tool in your toolbox for cultivating resilience. With the technology available today and the power of social media, there are countless communities you can join to find your support group. It may take some trial and error to find the right fit, but investing the time to find your tribe is well worth it.

Having people to cheer you on and bounce ideas off of is invaluable in the online business space.

This is why I've discovered my true calling in the form of collaborations where I can meet and connect with fellow entrepreneurs. The level of mutual support is truly remarkable, allowing everyone to benefit and grow together.

VII. Conclusion

My entrepreneurial journey has been full of challenges, setbacks, and moments of doubt. However, through resilience and determination (and a little bit of stubbornness), I've learned to overcome obstacles and continue moving forward.

Along the way, I've come to realize that building a business isn't just about me – it's about creating a legacy for my family. By pursuing my dreams and building something of my own, I'm not only providing for my loved ones but also showing them the power of hard work, perseverance, and resilience. Each step of this journey has been a lesson, and every setback has been an opportunity for growth.

As I continue on this path, I'm reminded that success isn't just measured in monetary value but in the impact we make and the legacy we leave for later generations.

Dr. Sonya A. McKinzie

Founder & CEO of ThriveHER Incorporated

https://www.linkedin.com/in/sonyamckinzie/
https://www.facebook.com/ThriveHERInc
https://www.instagram.com/thriveherinc/
www.thriveher.me

Dr. Sonya McKinzie is the CEO & Founder of ThriveHER Inc., a nonprofit organization established in 2016 to advocate for women affected by domestic violence and provide resources and tools to support them in taking their voices back. She is also a certified Trauma and Recovery Life Coach and has been honored with a Proclamation for ThriveHER Day in Brunswick, Georgia. Also, a best-selling author who has written and contributed to over twenty books, she is a visionary author for the forthcoming Blueprint of a ThriveHER Anthology. Sonya is most passionate about her daughter who is also an author and her overall faith in God. Dr. Sonya loves empowering women and girls to create HUGE footprints that will make a mark on the lives of others positively!

THE BECOMING OF A MOMPRENEUR: NAVIGATING BUSINESS, SETBACKS, SUCCESS, AND WHILE BEING AN INFLUENTIAL PARENT

By Dr. Sonya A. McKinzie

Well, hello, and welcome to my crazy yet invigorating world! I am a single mother to an amazing, thirteen-year-old miracle who just happens to carry my last name as her first name, McKinzie. I am also a Senior Customer Success Manager, Certified Trauma and Recovery Coach, author, and the CEO and Founder of ThriveHER Incorporated, a nonprofit organization that is in place to help women and girls break the chains of abuse and take back their voices from their abusers. Yes, I know what you are thinking – that sounds like a lot for one person – and I would have to say it depends on how you view it! I was raised by strong, hardworking, beautiful, black and brown women. It was through them that I acquired the tenacity and passion to strive for MORE than mediocrity.

Thinking over my past and present, my immediate thought process begins with my past experiences which were immersed with trials and tribulations. You see, I am a second-generation ThriveHER of domestic violence. Somewhere between discovering that I was broken and giving birth to my daughter, I discovered my overall purpose in life. It was also around that time that I reached the mountain top after much time spent in the desert. I learned God had guided me through the painful seasons so that I could appreciate and embrace "restoration" with gratitude and humility. Believe it or not, it took me nearly two decades after my second encounter with abuse to reach my healing destination. But … let me pump the brakes for a moment before jumping right into the meat and potatoes of this mompreneur story!

Let's start with, "Once Upon a Time," there was a story of a young lady who was raised in a small town by the name of Brunswick,

Georgia. In this town, many disparities limited employment and career opportunities, especially for young African American women "like me."

So maybe you are saying, "Wait, what?"

What does the part of the above statement "like me" represent? And what exactly does that have to do with being a mompreneur?

Personally speaking, it signifies a path that was less traveled in the early 2000s. You see, I was a dreamer who found herself navigating life heavily armed with insecurities coupled with a dreamer's versus a doer's mentality. In other words, I had big dreams but little motivation or knowledge on how to achieve and accomplish the goals associated with those dreams.

At the age of nineteen, I set my sights on college. I aspired to become a fashion designer, perhaps the next Versace who tailored to plus-sized women. Little did I know that the road ahead would be saturated with inequality, blood, sweat, tears, fierce competition, and unforeseen trials. I struggled with the curriculum, the projects, and the demands of keeping up with the "competition," better known as my classmates/peers to graduate. However, I made it through the storms, and like a phoenix from the ashes, I rose above my shortcomings and hard times. Nonetheless, it did not stop my desire to be rich and pampered like many of my roommates and peers.

After completing a scrupulous two-year Associate Degree program from what was classified as a prestigious college (which just happened to be in the heart of Buckhead, Georgia), I soon found myself eaten up by the big shark better known as the city of Atlanta. Unfortunately, I had to give up on my dreams and reluctantly returned to Brunswick, Georgia after graduation.

Upon returning home, I quickly learned that I was no longer a child, but a woman who had responsibilities and bills that had to be paid.

That is when reality kicked in, really kicked in! And that reality knocked me on my backside more times than a few. I later found myself juggling two dead-end jobs just to cover my rent. The corporate world remained distant, and my dreams seemed elusive. Yet, within this struggle, seeds of resilience were sown, and my journey from surviving to thriving began. Through setbacks, triumphs, and unexpected twists, I discovered my true calling and decided to reset my life's trajectory. This is where my story of transforming from survivor to ThriveHER began. It is within these very fibers that the testament of resilience, singlehood to single motherhood, and the pursuit of success against all odds fell to begin.

I remember the young lady who was diagnosed with infertility in her early twenties and how it felt to have yet another door slammed in my face, but this dream was different. It hollowed out my spirit and soul. It devastated me.

Fast-forward several years. I found myself living paycheck to paycheck, struggling to cover rent. By day, I worked as a vocational development instructor, supporting special needs middle and high school students. By night, I manned an answering service, assisting customers with account concerns, and dispatching services/calls during the 11:00 PM to 7:00 AM shift.

I was in a relationship with a man who said he loved and hated me in the same sentence; what followed consisted of emotional/physical abuse repressed with shame. This wasn't the future I had imagined, the idealized vision of success seemed distant, and the exposed reality was that entrepreneurship and motherhood would escape my existence forever. At least, in that season of life, I felt doom was my destination. Little did I know my abuser's incarceration would be my source to escape the pain and stagnated personal and professional lives that constrained me to remain in Brunswick, Georgia.

Upon relocating to Marietta, which was about twenty minutes away from downtown Atlanta, I secured my first job in corporate America as a customer service representative with an organization that would teach me more in five years than I had learned in the entire twenty-six years of my life. I found myself in a company that paid me double the salary of what I made at one of my jobs in Brunswick, and yet, I still felt there was a need to work a second job. That mentality did not last long. Even with making more money, I learned by accident that I was making less than my peers who happened to be Caucasian, younger, and less educated than I was. Nevertheless, I looked the other way as I was not equipped to have that conversation with the then-leadership team, at least, I did not think I was.

After working several years in the same role and taking on far more responsibilities than my peers, I inquired about a promotion and more money. After several inquiries throughout what would be six years, I became weary and tired of being reminded of my lack of college education and the limitations that it had on my desire to grow within the company. The frequent reminders of my restricted schooling weighed heavily on how I viewed my worth. I began to believe that I was not worthy of being more than an entry-level employee. Then, one day, I had a conversation with one of our leaders. I was encouraged to return to college and pursue a degree that would apply to my goals and aspirations – and I accepted the challenge. Over the next six years, I would pursue and obtain two associate's, two bachelor's, and two master's degrees which surpassed the education of many of the leaders within the company. Equipped with education, experience, time, and tenure, I inquired at each milestone (graduation) about being promoted, and like a horse and a dangling carrot, I received promotions; however, the promotions were like tiny little steps aligned to challenge my patience and my value, again. I went from being a Customer Service Rep (CSR) to a Senior CSR, to an assistant manager, to a manager. This process took twelve years.

Around year twelve, I discovered how very qualified I was and that my voice mattered whether those around me agreed or not. While I found myself pigeonholed, overlooked, disregarded, and disrespected, I remained with the company. Instead of allowing the actions of the leadership team to dismantle my grace, my value, and my self-respect. I worked hard to create an outlet that would allow me to do what I was passionate about while maintaining a job that would support me financially in achieving my goal of being a leader in my nonprofit organization.

You see, in 2010, I discovered I would be a mother, and in 2011, I graduated with my last Master's Degree in Communications with a focus on Public Relations three days before I gave birth to my daughter (the miracle that I was told would not happen). Four years after my daughter was born, I established the Women of Virtue Transitional Foundation and trademarked ThriveHER which would later become the focal point of my daughter and, more specifically, my legacy. The birthing of the organization was a direct reflection and connection to my experience with domestic and verbal abuse. My passion to breathe life into this entrepreneurial journey was founded on my desire to help women walk away from their abusers, take their voices back, and most importantly, break the generational curse of abuse that had trickled down from my mother to my lifeline. While my organization did not allow me to stop working a traditional job, it certainly equipped me with the tools and partnerships necessary to fight against domestic violence and advocate for women and girls affected by it.

Fast forward another five years, I am employed as a senior customer success manager, working for a manager who not only respects but also supports me and my aspirations. Additionally, I am also working on building up and out a for-profit arm under ThriveHER Movement Coaching and Counseling LLC, which has been registered with the state of Georgia as of March 2024. Amid this venture, I have also become an author who has participated and penned more than thirteen books as of today. This year has also presented an opportunity for me to stretch outside of my comfort zone to the not-so-comfortable zone, better known as "The Becoming of a Visionary Author."

On this journey, I have launched my first book collaboration "The Blueprint of a ThriveHER" which is pending release in early Summer 2024. This is yet another milestone in life that I consider no less than a blessing because this opportunity has created a space for me to generate an additional stream of income and to also work with and stand alongside women and men from backgrounds of all kinds.

When I chose to co-author in over twelve books, I did not realize it would lead to me becoming a visionary author; however, this journey of building an additional income as a visionary author is far more complex than that of being a co-author.

If becoming a visionary author is something you are thinking of, remember that creating an additional income by selling books online and establishing yourself as a visionary author can be an exciting venture but also a challenge. Below are some pertinent things to consider when launching as a visionary author:

1. **Identify Your Niche:** Determine the genre or subject matter where you have expertise or a unique perspective. This could be anything from self-help to science fiction.

2. **Write Your Book:** Aim for a minimum of 2,000 words to start. Ensure your content is engaging, well-researched, and offers value to your readers.

3. **Edit and Format:** Once your manuscript is complete, thoroughly edit it for clarity, grammar, and flow. Format it according to the requirements of the platforms you wish to sell on.

4. **Design a Cover:** A compelling cover can make a significant difference. Design one that reflects the essence of your book and catches the eye.

5. **Publish Online:** Use platforms like Amazon Kindle Direct Publishing, Barnes & Noble Press, or Apple Books to publish your ebook. You can also consider print-on-demand services for physical copies.

6. **Market Your Book:** Develop a marketing strategy that includes social media promotion, email marketing, and possibly a website or blog to build your author brand.

7. **Engage with Readers:** Build a community around your book. Engage with your readers through social media, book readings, and author Q&A sessions.

8. **Collect Reviews:** Encourage readers to leave reviews. Positive reviews can boost your book's visibility and credibility.

9. **Monitor Sales and Adjust:** Keep an eye on your sales. Use the data to adjust your marketing strategies and improve your book if necessary.

10. **Expand Your Catalog:** Continue writing and publishing more books to establish yourself as a thought leader in your niche and to create multiple streams of income.

Remember, being a visionary author is not just about writing; it's about connecting with your audience and offering them something that can enrich their lives or challenge their perspectives. Good luck on your author journey!

Aachieving success as a self-published author is a testament to one's commitment, dedication, creativity, and entrepreneurial spirit. It's a journey that begins with the seed of an idea and blossoms into a full-fledged literary enterprise. The self-publishing route empowers authors to take full control of the creative and marketing process, allowing them to establish a direct connection with their readership. This autonomy enables authors to make strategic decisions about their content, cover design, pricing, and promotional activities, tailoring each aspect to their target audience's preferences.

The digital age has revolutionized the publishing industry, providing tools and platforms that facilitate the distribution and promotion of ebooks and print-on-demand paperbacks. Authors can now reach a global audience without the need for traditional publishing gatekeepers. Success in this arena is measured not only by sales but also by the ability to build a loyal fan base, receive constructive feedback, and continuously improve one's craft.

Selling books becomes an additional stream of income that, while passive at times, requires ongoing effort in terms of marketing and audience engagement. Successful self-published authors often wear multiple hats such as becoming adept at social media marketing, email list building, and networking with other authors and industry professionals. They understand the importance of a well-crafted book description, a captivating cover, and a strategic pricing model. Moreover, they recognize the value of garnering reviews which serve as social proof and can significantly influence potential readers' purchasing decisions.

Financial success varies among self-published authors with some achieving modest supplemental income while others generate substantial revenue, rivaling traditionally published authors. The key is to maintain a consistent output of quality content, establish a recognizable brand, and adapt to the ever-changing market trends. Diversifying one's portfolio by writing in different genres or creating series can also attract a wider audience and increase sales potential.

Success as a self-published author is multifaceted, combining the art of writing with the science of marketing. It offers a rewarding path for those who are passionate about sharing their stories and willing to embrace the challenges of entrepreneurship. With perseverance, adaptability, and a focus on delivering value to readers, self-publishing can become a lucrative and fulfilling additional stream of income.

So, the questions are flowing – how, when, why, and how are you doing all these things AND still working in corporate America?

Since I am being transparent, I will add, that I do not care to always work for another company, but there are process steps that must be achieved before jumping ship. You see, transitioning from corporate America to becoming a successful mompreneur involves deliberate steps and tactical planning. Some people opt to JUMP. However, I chose the following road map to guide me towards mastering momprenuership:

1. **Self-Assessment and Vision Clarity:**

   o Reflect on your passions, strengths, and long-term goals. What drives you? What impact do you want to create? Define your vision for your business and life beyond the corporate world.

2. **Skill Enhancement and Knowledge Acquisition:**

   o Identify the skills needed for your entrepreneurial venture. Consider taking courses, attending workshops, or seeking mentorship to enhance your expertise.

   o Learn about business fundamentals, marketing, finance, and operations. Understand the industry you plan to enter.

3. **Financial Preparation:**

   o Build a financial safety net. Save enough to cover personal expenses during the transition phase.
   o Create a budget that accounts for business expenses, marketing, and initial investments.

4. **Business Idea and Market Research:**

   o Brainstorm business ideas aligned with your passion and skills. Research market trends and identify gaps.
   o Understand your target audience, competitors, and potential customer needs.

5. **Business Plan Development:**

   o Draft a comprehensive business plan. Include your mission, vision, target market, value proposition, marketing strategy, and financial projections.
   o Define your unique selling points (USPs) and competitive advantage.

6. **Legal and Administrative Setup:**

   o Register your business entity (LLC, sole proprietorship, etc.). Obtain necessary licenses and permits.
   o Consult legal professionals to ensure compliance with local regulations.

7. **Networking and Building Relationships:**

   o Attend industry events, conferences, and networking sessions. Connect with other entrepreneurs, mentors, and potential clients.
   o Leverage social media platforms to build your brand and expand your network.

8. **Time Management and Prioritization:**

   o Balancing a corporate job and entrepreneurship requires effective time management. Create a schedule that allocates time for both.

   o Prioritize tasks based on urgency and importance.

9. **Gradual Transition:**

   o Consider a phased approach. Start your business as a side hustle while maintaining your corporate job.

   o As your business gains traction, gradually reduce your corporate hours.

10. **Marketing and Branding:**

   o Develop a strong brand identity. Create a professional website, business cards, and social media profiles.

   o Use content marketing, social media, and networking to promote your business.

11. **Financial Stability and Risk Mitigation:**

   o Ensure your business generates consistent income before quitting your corporate job.

   o Have an emergency fund to handle unexpected challenges.

12. **Mindset Shift and Resilience:**

   o Embrace the mindset of an entrepreneur. Be prepared for setbacks, adaptability, and persistence.

   o Surround yourself with a supportive community.

Embarking on the journey of a mompreneur is a unique blend of nurturing a family and cultivating a business. It's a role that demands a harmonious balance between the tenderness of motherhood and the tenacity of entrepreneurship. To thrive in this dual capacity, patience is paramount. It is the quiet strength that allows a mompreneur to weather the slow periods of business growth and the developmental stages of her children. Patience fosters a nurturing environment where both family and business can flourish.

Humility is another cornerstone of success for a mompreneur. It keeps one grounded and open to learning from every experience, whether it's a parenting challenge or business setback. A humble approach invites collaboration and support from others which is vital in juggling the complexities of motherhood and entrepreneurship.

Creativity is the lifeblood of a mompreneur. It's not just about artistic expression; it's about innovative problem-solving, resourcefulness, and the ability to see possibilities where others see obstacles. Creativity turns mundane tasks into exciting opportunities and propels the business forward with fresh ideas and solutions.

Time management is a critical skill for a mompreneur. It's about prioritizing tasks, setting realistic goals, and creating a schedule that accommodates the demands of family life and the rigors of business. Wise time management means knowing when to delegate when to say no, and when to take a moment for oneself.

Organizing and compartmentalizing commitments and tasks are essential strategies. They help maintain focus and prevent the overwhelm that can come from wearing multiple hats. By categorizing responsibilities and setting clear boundaries, a mompreneur can transition smoothly between roles, giving her full attention to the task at hand.

Dedication is the fuel that drives a mompreneur. It's the unwavering commitment to her vision, the relentless pursuit of her goals, and the steadfast belief in her ability to make a difference. Dedication keeps a mompreneur going, even when the path is fraught with challenges.

Emotional resilience is perhaps the most crucial trait of all. It's the ability to bounce back from disappointments, to remain optimistic in the face of adversity, and to maintain emotional equilibrium amidst the highs and lows of business and family life. Emotional resilience ensures that a mompreneur can lead her business and family with confidence and grace.

In essence, being a successful mompreneur is about embodying these qualities and applying them to the intricate dance of raising a family and running a business. It's a journey that requires a heart full of passion, a mind brimming with ideas, and a spirit resilient enough to embrace each day's challenges and triumphs.

Finally, if you're considering the path of being a mompreneur, take a paragraph or two from my chapter: be patient, have grace and mercy for not only you but others, embrace your strength, seek knowledge, don't be afraid to fail (remember to brush yourself off and up), and strive to build a thriving business that you are passionate about while loving and nurturing your family and always keep God at the center of all things that you do.

As shared before, being a mompreneur is a role that symbolizes the blending of nurturing a family and growing a business. It's a path that requires a delicate balance, unwavering dedication, and a strategic approach to managing time and resources. Success in this endeavor is not just about financial gain but also about personal fulfillment, growth, and the ability to make a positive impact on both your family and the community.

Personally speaking, my journey as a mompreneur has been paved with trials but it has also been lined with opportunities. The wealth of resources available today—books that provide wisdom, programs that offer guidance, blogs that share experiences, podcasts that deliver insights, and supportive communities that encourage collaboration—can be instrumental to your success. These resources serve as a compass, helping you navigate the complexities of entrepreneurship while maintaining the warmth and responsibilities of motherhood.

Remember, every mompreneur's story is unique, and your narrative will be a tapestry woven from your experiences, lessons learned, and milestones achieved. Your story has the power to inspire others to follow their dreams, persevere through adversity, and celebrate every victory, no matter how small.

As you write the chapters of your own mompreneur journey, be reminded that patience, creativity, and resilience are your buddies. Press forward during the learning process, cherish the moments with your family, and let your entrepreneurial spirit soar. Your story is not just about achieving success; it's about inspiring others to believe that they, too, can achieve their dreams while creating a harmonious balance between family and business.

I pray that your story (journey) will be a flare of confidence and a testament to the fact that with passion, willpower, and the right resources, success as a mompreneur is not just a possibility—it's a reality waiting to be realized.

As a mompreneur, you must have profound courage and unwavering determination. It's a path that intertwines the nurturing love of a mother with the bold spirit of an entrepreneur. In this pursuit, it's essential to remember that your dreams are the wings upon which your future soars. **Never give up** on these aspirations, for they are the seeds from which the fruits of your labor will one day bloom.

While striving for professional success, it's equally important to weave a tapestry of **self-care and self-love** into the fabric of your daily life. This isn't just an act of indulgence—it's a vital strategy for sustainability. By taking the time to replenish your well-being, you ensure that you have the energy and vitality to give the best of yourself to both your family and your business.

Self-care can manifest in many forms: a quiet moment with a cup of tea before the children wake, a brisk walk in the fresh air to clear your mind, or even a few pages of a book that ignites your imagination. Self-love is about recognizing your worth, celebrating your accomplishments, and forgiving yourself for the inevitable imperfections that come with being human.

The vessel of your spirit must be filled before you can pour into others. By nurturing your own spirit and well-being, you become a reservoir of strength and resilience. This balance is the cornerstone of a mompreneur's success—it allows you to chase your dreams without running on empty, to face challenges with grace, and to embrace victories with joy. So, carry on with heart and hustle, but also with kindness towards yourself, for it is in this harmony that true success is found.

At the heart of every mompreneur's journey is the profound truth that being a mom comes first and being an entrepreneur follows. This beautiful balance is the essence of your strength and success. As a mother, you are the first teacher, primary nurturer, and constant source of love and stability in your child's life. Your entrepreneurial spirit is an extension of the same love—a desire to build something that fulfills you and secures your family's future.

Embrace this dual role with pride and confidence knowing that the patience, wisdom, and resilience you exhibit as a mother are the very traits that will propel you forward in business. Each day, as you navigate the challenges and triumphs of motherhood, you are also setting an extraordinary example for your children—an example of determination, hard work, and the pursuit of dreams.

As a mother, the legacy you create extends far beyond the confines of your own life. Your children, the silent observers of your strength, determination, and grace, are learning invaluable lessons with each step you take. They are absorbing the essence of perseverance, the beauty of dreaming big, and the importance of making a positive impact. Remember, the path you tread is not walked alone. It is illuminated by the eyes that watch you with admiration and the hearts that are inspired by your journey. You are not just raising children; you are nurturing future leaders, thinkers, and dreamers. The legacy you build as a mompreneur is a tapestry of love, ambition, and inspiration—a gift to your children and all those who find courage in your story. **Carry this knowledge close to your heart,** for it is the most profound and enduring success you can achieve.

So, hold fast to this truth: your role as a mom is the foundation upon which your entrepreneurial dreams are built. It's a reminder that in the intricate dance of balancing family and business, your heart as a mother guides you, and your actions as an entrepreneur inspire. Let this be your encouragement, your beacon of light, as you continue to grow and thrive in both incredibly important roles. **You are a mom first, a preneur next, and an inspiration always.**

Tanya Kravcenko

Chartered Accountant, Author

https://www.linkedin.com/company/tanyakravcenko/
https://www.facebook.com/TheJellybeanTheory
https://www.instagram.com/tanyakravcenkonz/
www.tanyakravcenko.com

Tanya Kravcenko is a chartered accountant with a passion for financial literacy and has more than 20 years of industry experience. After spending her career supporting small businesses and entrepreneurs, Tanya noticed a significant gap in financial literacy among younger (and even older) generations. This inspired her to develop coaching sessions to empower people with the tools to make positive life choices and reach their full potential.

"IT IS WHAT IT IS."

By Tanya Kravcenko

This was my nephew's (Mark) favourite saying whenever anyone asked him how he was doing. He passed away on 2/3/24 from cancer at the age of 33.

So many times I would question and try to change what "it" is. I am not sure if I could be that strong when loved ones looked me in the eye and said how sorry they were for the journey I was going on. I would suggest to Mark healthy alternatives so that he could live longer, but he knew that he had a terminal disease and it was spreading fast. The doctors initially gave him 48 hours, but he proved them wrong and kept strong for 10 months. That is why his nickname is Marky Sparky; no matter what he always had a spark.

His other words of wisdom for me were, "Aunty, sometimes you make your life complicated." I would look back at him and think, Jeepers, you are the one whose life is so complicated right now, having to hear doctors say to you that you have a terminal disease, but you would try this treatment or that treatment to get an opportunity to live one more day."

Mark was such a wise man at such a young age, but out of everyone, he taught me what life is all about. It is about having the courage to stand up to whatever you are dealt with to just say to yourself "It is what it is" and not overthink the situation.

Sometimes you cannot change the cards that you have been dealt, but you can change what you want to do with them. You can keep them or throw them away. On October 1, 2015, I decided to leave my daughter's father. He had a mental illness called Bipolar Disorder which left him in states of depression where he could not function as a human for weeks, and then there were times when he felt that he was famous and had many companies and employees.

The one thing that I will be forever grateful for from this man is that out of all the men in my life, he was the only one who would have a child with me, so my dream to be called Mum could come true. For no medical reason, I was never able to conceive a child naturally, but then destiny happened and our daughter came into our life purely by chance.

At the time, we were looking at fostering a girl through Child Youth and Family, and a friend rang me and asked if I would like to adopt her future granddaughter. Of course, I said yes I would adopt the child. There was no reason to say no. I knew the mother and knew she had taken good care of her pregnancy, so the risk of having a child that was affected by alcohol or drugs was out of the question. The girl we were looking at fostering was from a mum who had already had several children and there was a chromosome missing, so all of her children to date had mental health issues, so there was a chance the girl we were looking at would have mental health issues also. I had to decide if I wanted to carry on with the fostering process with CYFS or adopt my friend's granddaughter. I wanted to have both, but my partner was not keen on being a parent to both, so I chose my friend's granddaughter.

Four months later our daughter was given to us. You cannot explain how it feels when a child is put into your arms. The look of innocence on their face and then the sudden thought that you are responsible for this little person's life until they can make the big decisions for themselves. Reality hits when you are holding them and that first meconium faeces appears. That was my first job as her "mum." To change the meconium nappy. Thankfully, I had a sister when I was 12, and I had nieces and nephews, so changing a nappy was not a problem at all, but no one told me about the meconium one. Seventeen years later I can say now that was just the beginning of all the "fun" things I have done as a mother.

The wise words my partner told me when I was learning how to be a mum was "Don't forget who you were before you were a mum, remember who Tanya was." I started doing what I loved, and that was playing netball. The training was on Wednesdays and the games were on Saturdays, allowing me to feel like myself and be happy doing what I loved while being around other females who were juggling kids and life. Our daughter would come down to the netball courts and watch me play and cheer me on. Then I played touch rugby and the same thing happened again. I was also a long-distance runner, so at the end of each event, I would have my support crew there celebrating my completion of the half marathon. Now our daughter is an enthusiastic horse rider and it is my turn to cheer her on. I passed those words of wisdom on to my daughter to never forget to do what you love.

When I became a solo mum, I had no idea how to live my life. I was a caregiver for my partner for a long time and now I had all this time available to run my accounting practice, look after the "farm" where our daughter's horse would graze, and again try to find "Tanya" as a single person. I had been in relationships for 30 years. I had no idea how to be single. I was 49 at the time – about to enter my fifth decade. The single dating apps were another world. Back in my day, we met people at bars, work, through friends, or just by chance, but now I was encouraged by my nephews to use Tinder or Find Someone or Be2. The hardest time was the evenings when the house was all quiet, and I would get bored talking to the no-brainers on the apps and decided to make better use of my time. So, I started writing my book The Jellybean Theory. The theory is that if I gave you a jar of jellybeans and said, "This is all the money you will have in your lifetime, what would you do with it?

Here I was navigating life on my own at 49 asking myself, "Now what?" I had a daughter with a horse, a business, a little farm, a boat (my sanity saver), a dog called Yuki that my brother gave me before he moved to

Brazil, a dog called Rufus (who is a bit of a doofus), a flock of sheep (my brother kindly gave me), a cat called Kimba and a goat called Daisy.

I looked at my friends who were "happily married," "successful in their careers," and "great at parenting" and thought, "How do I do that but without the marriage bit?"

So over two consistent nights, I wrote my book – three thousand words each night, and then finished the rest of the book within three months and had it published. I then took the book to my high school and asked a very wise old man on the board what he thought about it. He said it was great, but take the word "sex" out of it if I wanted him to sponsor the payment of 100 books for the pupils. I laughed inside and thought how many times the kids must see the word "sex" on TV, on TikTok, on Instagram, etc, but I did it because I valued his contribution and maybe it was something that did not need to be in my book.

Then I was given the opportunity to introduce myself to a classroom of thirty 16,17, and 18-year-olds and tell them my story of how I became an author and someone who is passionate about money and happiness. After three hours, I left the classroom feeling I had achieved something and I had done what I was meant to do for the rest of my life.

I kept my accounting practice going for two more years, but then in January 2023, I decided to follow my dream to teach people the meaning of money and happiness through my story.

In my first marriage, I was lucky to share the winnings in the first division of lotto and we had enough money to buy our first home in a prestigious area. Unfortunately, my husband wanted to party for the rest of his days all day but I wanted more than that, so we separated.

Then, I met husband number two who taught me the most important thing in life and that was "the most limiting factor we have is time." It is so true. We can make as much money as we like but we have only one lifetime, one day, one week, one month, one year. And when you break life down like this and live every day as if it is your last, you soon build your ultimate life.

My second husband and I separated after nine years of marriage. I was devastated. He was my soul mate, and I did not understand what a nervous breakdown was. Unfortunately, he let work rule his life and didn't know what balance was. I fortunately always exercised and remembered to play with my friends. I also worked hard in my career but from an early stage in my career, I learned how to work smart. I had no idea about the gift I was given when I chose a career as a chartered accountant. I could walk into businesses and know instantly what needed to be done to turn them around and make them very successful. I have worked for the richest man in New Zealand and he was a great teacher of what makes a good business. Best products, best people, best systems and services, and a happy work environment. It's that simple. When I ran my own practice, I tried for 10 years to find the best person to work beside me and she did right until I closed my practice in January 2023. This person did not have an accounting qualification, but she understood numbers and systems and processes, and most of all she knew how to relate to my clients. Relationships are the most important skill in life. To get the best out of anything you need to have a good relationship. Even with my daughter who is now 17, I am teaching her what a positive relationship is in all aspects of her life. Unfortunately, social media does not do this; it is the real-life interactions that teach you the fundamentals of life.

Hence why I have recreated my career as a teacher of financial literacy and mindset. My new brand encompasses my beliefs as a person and also includes my experience in the financial world. While I was in public practice, I saw that 98% of my clients could not read their financial statements, but they were in control of the most important thing in their lives – their money. And I would experience tearful meetings with my clients as to why they could not meet their financial obligations. I wanted people to have a positive experience with their businesses and their cash flow choices. I would ask my clients every year if everything was going the way they wanted it to be and also if they were happy with life, most accountants would not have this heart-centered conversation. Most accountants like to talk about the numbers and that's it because that is all the client can afford to pay for. I was never all about the money. I cared about my clients, and it hit hard when one client committed suicide because he thought he did not have enough money. I just wish to this day we could have had a conversation about what he was thinking because it was not true. His business was starting to turn around and the money was beginning to flow, but the expectations that were put upon him of what a "happy" life is were not within his bank balance. Happiness is not defined by a bank balance. I am probably the only chartered accountant who will say it is not all about the money.

This is where society has gone wrong – we have not put the people first. Banks are making huge profits at the cost of people losing their homes and not being able to put food on the table or clothes on their backs. I would like the whole world to have a complete reset and go back to the days when we lived like a "village." Where we supported and cared about each other. Where food was shared with laughter and love. Love is the most important currency in the world.

Every time I am going through a "crisis," the most amazing people walk into my life and show me the sunshine again. All by just talking, listening, laughing, and maybe sharing a cup of tea and my favourite – a piece of cake. It is the simple things that matter. Now I have lost both parents, I wish I could share a meal with both of them, but thank goodness both of them taught me what good food was. My dad being of Yugoslavian descent, was very passionate about making the most of sharing special moments with family and friends around food, music, conversation (sometimes big political debates), and laughter. Being a mechanic, he built the best barbeque which could cook his signature meat patties for a family of five kids and Grandad who lived with us. Mum was very resourceful when Dad would organise surprise gatherings at our house and Mum would go to the garden and create salads for everyone. Money was not surplus, but love was. Everyone was always made welcome in our house and food was always found somewhere.

In my difficult financial times as a solo mother, I reflected on the gifts my parents taught me, and every time I needed money, it would just appear. I was running my accounting practice, a seven-acre farm, looking after a daughter who loved owning a pony, and there was still money left to have friends over to share a meal with. When I was saving to go to Europe when I was 21, I learned quickly how to teach my friends what a potluck dinner was. My partner made homebrew, so there was plenty of beer – sometimes not that nice tasting, but at 21, you are not that fussy. My partner and I always managed to find the money to have dinner parties at our house, and we both saved for our big OE so I could meet my dad's family. Unfortunately, my dad passed away when I was 21 from a heart attack. That was the biggest wake-up call in my life. My dad was only 56. I said to myself – is that it? Is that how long I have had my dad? I was so angry and grieved for about a year. But saving to go to Europe to see his family for the first time was what kept me going. Travel has always been my passion. To see how others live, what food they eat, what buildings they live in, and how they navigate around the planet. I just loved visiting Venice and seeing how they used water as their form of transport. I am a keen boaty and just love using my boat to venture around the Hauraki Gulf. I also love to catch a snapper for dinner.

That is what life is about – making the best of whatever is in front of you. In January 2023 when I moved from my "forever" home, I found it hard to move back to a residential area. The bonus was my mum lived two minutes away, so whenever I got busy in the kitchen, she would just drive around and taste my samples. Mum got busy in the kitchen too and made me heaps of relish and pickles. She was so happy to be able to drive around and give me her treats. When I lived 30 minutes away, she could not do that as due to her health she was restricted. I was so happy to see my mum laughing and talking happily in the four months I had with her before she passed away in August last year. She loved her garden and would delight in telling me what I should and shouldn't do in mine. My daughter adopted a love for gardening too and her Nana was so happy to see her granddaughter plant her first rose garden. My mum's name was Rosemary, and some people called her Rose, so a rose garden was definitely meant to be planted. We now have a seat that was once at my mum's house where we can sit and look at the roses and remember the stories of the happy times when we would sit at our Mum's house looking at her beautiful garden.

The program I am creating for kids in schools is based on dreams -, in business, we call them goals. But as a child, I had the most amazing dreams. One was to own a Ferrari (I just love the colour red). At present, I have a red MX5 which I drive like a Ferrari. It is 34 years old and has created a lot of lasting memories. One was where I would have to look after my three nephews and I would put little Mark on the floor, big Misha would sit on the passenger seat, and middle child Paul would lie across the back shelf. Luckily, I was never seen by a policeman, but that is what I had to do to get the boys to their rugby training. Thankfully, their parents were unaware of how their aunty was "looking after" them.

I want people to remember to think about their dreams/goals and how they can be made possible. One day I will own a Ferrari, and it will be red and hopefully, it will be before I am 60. I will own a farm again so that my daughter can graze her horse in her backyard and have an arena for her to teach others how to ride. My daughter is now of the age where she can contribute to that financial journey, as she is about to start her career as a dog groomer. Our passion for dogs is the same – we have three little darlings. I always wanted a big family, and they are definitely our family.

The biggest lesson I have learned in life is to never give up on your dreams, no matter what. Hurdles are thrown our way, and it is how we respond to them that matters. Yes, there will be pain and sorrow, but the laughter and joy can overrule those feelings if you just keep on looking at the sun. COVID was a difficult time for so many people and a lot of loss happened. There was money and lives lost. The money you can replace. The lives you cannot.

This is why I am so passionate about focusing on what you want your dream life to be. I always wanted to be a mum and she was given to me. I always wanted to be in charge of my time, so I started my accounting practice. I always wanted to be of service to people, but I did not want that way of being to own me. I learned very quickly last year that I needed to be of service to myself first. To do what I loved and stop being the people pleaser. It was a hard lesson to learn, but I can now say I learned it. Without my mum being so near to me and the cups of tea and yummy food we shared, I would not have healed so quickly and she knew she could leave Earth knowing that my daughter and I were in a happy place after being treated so badly by so-called professionals like lawyers, real estate agents, politicians, business owners, and the police. The explanation of this comment is for another story on another day. The world is not ready to hear that story yet. I never in my dreams believed such a practice happened in New Zealand, but unfortunately, the bad way of doing business is all over the world in the name of greed.

There is enough food, land, and clothing for everyone to be comfortable. That is why I am building my "school of life" in

Beachlands this year. Most of the school will be on the Cloud as that is how we learn now. I took for granted what my parents taught me and thought that everyone knew how to cook, clothe themselves, and find shelter until I taught at Manurewa High School and saw the students respond to my book with confusion. The word invest was not in their vocabulary and the ability to set a goal was not in their understanding. It took five adults to support thirty 16 – 18-year-olds to set one goal each.

I know that to achieve a goal you need a "village" around you. I was always fortunate enough to find a "village" because my Mum taught me one important thing in life. That it is okay to ask a question – you can get one of two answers, a yes or a no. The "no" answer is always the fun one because I always come back with the word "Why?" Every parent hates this word as it challenges their reasoning. When I wanted a tight short mini skirt at the age of 15 and my dad said no, I asked him so many times "Why?" He had no reason. He did not know how to explain to his daughter that was not what he wanted me to wear because it would attract attention from potential undesirable boys. So after my persistence and advising my dad that he had to let me make my own choices, Mum being the good sewer that she was, did make me a nice denim skirt. My mum was cleverer than all of us, as she knew denim shrunk when you washed it, so after the first wash it no longer fit and that was the end of that argument, as at that time I was in a position to pay for my clothing from my part time job and I was not willing to risk a worn only once denim skirt is made.

My daughter learned this principle too around the age of three. I would give her a two-dollar coin each week to go to her favourite shop called Coin Save. My daughter loved this shop and would try to bring the whole shop home every time we went in there. So I took the liberty of teaching her the value of a number. I would tell her to look for something in the shop with a two on it. Sofia was very clever and would come back with a toy with a three or four on it. So I took the opportunity to teach her about saving and told her if she kept the two-dollar coin in her purse this week, then when she got another two-dollar coin next week, she could buy the four-dollar toy she wanted. So she did that. This went on for a few months until she discovered that each toy would not last very long, no matter how much she spent on it, so the Coin Shop soon became her least favourite shop.

When she was five, she fell in love with the Scholastic book flyer and wanted so many books. I quickly set her a budget of $10 per week. $3 was for books, $3 was for toys, $3 was for saving and $1 was for whatever she wanted to buy. Usually lollies. Being the clever deal buyer that she was, she would get the most books on each flyer and learn the meaning of the word "sale" really fast. Also by giving her $1 of freedom each week, she learned that $1 can buy a very small amount of all her "wants".

At the age of eight, I gave her a $200 clothing budget each season. By this time, she really knew what "sale" meant and also the best store to get the best "sales" which was Kmart. For a child who wanted so many items of clothing when she thought Mum had this magic card that would just keep on giving to a child who learned that the card was not limitless and to hold $200 was a powerful way to show her how limiting $200 can be. But Sofia was able to buy everything she "needed" each season and have money left over to choose what she wanted.

This is what money should be for – to get everything you need and also give you the freedom of choice. When I did this example with a class of 16 – 18 year olds they had trouble understanding the concept of a budget. I want to teach the kids before they go into the workforce what a budget is. The value of a number and how it can give you freedom if you use money in a positive way.

To understand that you can afford shelter, food, and clothing no matter what. It is a matter of being as resourceful as my parents were.

They always found the measure to shelter, clothe, and feed whoever came to our house. Sometimes, people would repay them with money, but lots of times people would just take what they "needed" and forget to say thank you or give whatever money they had. In the world of unconditional love, this is okay. When you are giving, you feel so much better than when you are receiving.

The world is about what is in it for me now. I enjoy asking people what can I do for you? I was a person who could not tell someone the answer. Now I can, and now I can open my financial literacy school, provide a home for my daughter, myself, and our fur babies, and plan my trips to travel around the world.

Thank you for reading my story about my life. I would love to hear your story one day about your dreams and how they came true. Remember there is always a solution and there will always be challenges. Believing in yourself and knowing that you can find a village to support you, will get you to where you "need" to be. Like the Rolling Stones song says, "No you can't always get what you want. But if you try sometimes, you'll find you get what you need."

Tanya Kravcenko

Tauni Maya

CEO of Babies Made with Love

www.linkedin.com/in/taunimaya
https://www.instagram.com/realfertilitytalk/
www.babiesmadewithlove.com
www.realfertilitytalk.com

Tauni has over a decade of experience in the fertility field helping people from all around the world to become parents. She is the CEO of Babies Made with Love Egg Donation and Surrogacy which was selected as the top surrogacy agency of 2023 by Healthcare Business Magazine. She is using her platform Real Fertility Talk: Journey to Parenthood to document her journey and struggles to become a mom and help inform and educate people on infertility and the different paths to parenthood. Tauni is also the founder of Baby Wish Foundation helping people to become parents through grants and partnerships! Tauni has been an entrepreneur since she was six years old and hope to inspire and help women to become badass bosses!

SERIAL ENTREPRENEUR, INFERTILITY AND MOTHERHOOD - CELEBRATING SMALL WINS: WHY IT'S IMPORTANT TO RECOGNIZE YOUR ACCOMPLISHMENTS AS A MOM BOSS

By Tauni Maya

As an entrepreneur since the age of six, I never thought that the most challenging job I have undertaken would be becoming a mom. As a fertility expert, I am well aware of the difficulties of becoming pregnant, but I never thought I would personally experience it. I was not prepared for the challenges that came after becoming a mother - juggling work, motherhood, and dealing with postpartum depression, anxiety, and rage.

In our society, there are certain topics like infertility, postpartum mental health, and the challenges of motherhood that are considered taboo. We often feel pressured to conform to media and social media standards and strive for perfection while juggling multiple responsibilities. Despite my initial confidence about handling pregnancy, motherhood, and running a business, I soon realized that I was not as prepared as I thought. However, with time, I learned to celebrate small wins and acknowledge my progress! I am not the same woman I was before I became a mom, and I am not going to be the same entrepreneur I was before.

When my son was born, I felt overwhelmed with the feeling of being reborn. I told everyone I felt like I didn't just give birth to my baby; I gave birth to a new me as well. I felt my whole world changed, not just physically or mentally, but my priorities, my brain, everything. I went from trying to conquer the world, trying to be the best agency, and taking Zoom meetings in my hospital room to only caring about my little newborn and dropping the ball here and there with my business.

The more little mistakes here and there I made, the more stressed and depressed I got. So many moments, I doubted myself and questioned why I wanted to become a mom. I asked myself if I went from Boss Bitch to Boss, Bitch! There were so many moments of self-doubt and deep depression, and that's why I'm here to remind you to celebrate the small wins and recognize those mom-boss achievements.

As a mom and entrepreneur, whether you are new to the game or experienced, it's easy to get so caught up in the day-to-day tasks of running a business and taking care of your family that you forget to celebrate your accomplishments - small or big! However, taking the time to recognize and appreciate your small wins is crucial for maintaining motivation, staying positive, and building momentum. Let's dive deeper into why celebrating small wins is so important.

1. **Boosts Confidence:** Celebrating small wins helps boost confidence and self-esteem. When you achieve a small goal, you feel a sense of accomplishment and pride in your work. This feeling of success helps you develop a positive self-image and belief in your abilities. It reminds you that you're capable of achieving great things, no matter how small they may seem.

2. **Motivates You:** Celebrating small wins motivates you to keep going. Acknowledging and celebrating your achievements provides the encouragement and momentum you need to tackle more considerable challenges and achieve more significant victories. It's essential to remember that progress is made up of small steps, and celebrating each step helps keep you motivated and focused on your goals.

3. **Builds Resilience:** When you celebrate small wins, you build resilience. You learn to bounce back from setbacks and keep pushing forward, even when things get tough. Recognizing your accomplishments helps you develop a growth mindset,

seeing setbacks as opportunities to learn and grow rather than failures. This resilience will serve you well in both your personal and professional life.

4. **Fosters Gratitude:** Celebrating small wins fosters gratitude. It reminds you to be thankful for your progress and the people who've helped you along the way. It's essential to acknowledge the contributions of others in your successes, whether it's your family, friends, or team members. Gratitude helps to create a positive and supportive environment where everyone feels valued and appreciated.

5. **Encourages Positivity:** Finally, celebrating small wins encourages positivity. It helps you focus on the good things in your life rather than the negative. Celebrating your accomplishments creates a positive feedback loop, where you feel good about yourself, making achieving more success easier. This positivity can also be contagious, spreading to those around you and creating a positive work and home environment. So, whether you've landed a new client, completed a project, or simply managed to get through a busy day without losing your mind, take the time to celebrate your small wins. You deserve it, mom-boss!

The feeling of having to choose between being a mom and an entrepreneur can be overwhelming and confusing. As a mom, your priority is to provide your family with love and care, while as an entrepreneur, you want to build a successful business. However, it's important to understand that you don't have to choose one over the other. It's possible to balance both and create a fulfilling life as a mompreneur.

Balancing motherhood and entrepreneurship requires the right mindset and support system. It's essential to set realistic expectations for yourself and your business. Don't be afraid to ask for help when necessary, whether from family or friends or by hiring an assistant. Delegating tasks can free up your time and allow you to focus on what's important.

Celebrating small wins along the way is crucial for maintaining motivation and staying positive. Whether landing a new client, completing a project, or simply getting through a busy day without losing your mind, take the time to acknowledge your accomplishments. By recognizing and appreciating your small wins, you're reminding yourself that you can achieve great things, no matter how small they seem.

Balancing motherhood and entrepreneurship takes dedication and perseverance. You may face setbacks and challenges along the way, but it's important to stay focused on your goals and keep pushing forward. Remember that progress is made up of small steps, and each step is an achievement worth celebrating.

I remember when my son was a newborn and celebrating the little things like making time to brush my teeth and wash my face. Then there was a moment when my son was five months old, I was on the cover of a magazine, but I was feeling so depressed about not accomplishing one of my goals - starting my own podcast just because someone I knew launched their podcast. I felt like I was falling behind in my career plan. My friend reminded me that I needed to celebrate this big win. I was on the cover of a prestigious healthcare magazine after being recognized as the best surrogacy agency in the US. It took this major event for me to learn to not compare my entrepreneurship journey with someone else's journey. Even though I have not launched my podcast yet, it does not mean I can't celebrate other wins. So remember, big or small, we should acknowledge it all! Finally, had a chance to take a shower and do a little self-care. Hooray! Able to leave your newborn for the first time to attend a work event? Let's do a little celebratory dance!

In conclusion, you don't have to choose between being a mom and an entrepreneur. With the right mindset, support system, and dedication, you can balance both and live a fulfilling life. Be bold and ask for help, set realistic expectations, and celebrate your small wins along the way. Balancing motherhood and entrepreneurship is possible, and you can succeed as a mompreneur.

Tiffany Hernandez

Founder of Tender Heart Ministries

https://www.linkedin.com/in/tlghernandez
https://www.facebook.com/tiffany.lynn.5011
https://www.instagram.com/tenderheartministries
https://linktr.ee/ultimatehomeschool

Meet Tiffany Hernandez, a dedicated mother of three and visionary founder of Tender Heart Ministries. Graduating in Interior Design, she courageously followed God's calling to homeschooling and ministry, serving her community with passion and purpose. Through Tender Heart Ministries, Tiffany blends her love for education and faith, offering support and guidance both locally and online. As the host of "The Ultimate Homeschool Community Podcast" and through coaching services, she empowers families to create enriching educational experiences at home and within learning communities. While inspiring others to embrace ministry leadership, Tiffany has a compassionate heart and a dedication to service that remains a beacon of inspiration. Her story embodies faith, family, and the transformative power of answering God's call. Tiffany's commitment showcases the impact one person can have on a community, sparking a ripple effect of embracing one's calling with love and purpose. Despite adversity, she attributes all the blessings of life to God's grace, finding strength in faith to serve those who cross her path.

FROM MESS TO MINISTRY- DISCOVERING HOW GOD'S PLAN IS GREATER

By Tiffany Hernandez

My story is like untangling a ball of yarn - so many intertwined elements! This chapter won't cover it all, but I'll do my best to give you a glimpse into its complexity. My journey has been quite a whirlwind of career experiences, motherhood challenges, entrepreneurial pitfalls, and triumphs all knotted together. I'll share a few highlights, hoping they'll help you on your own journey, and help you see you are not alone in your own journey. As I always say, take what works for you and leave the rest. Not every piece of advice suits everyone, but you will find some golden nuggets along the way to stash in your toolbox. Let's dive in and uncover those gems together!

The Early Years

I've always had a driven attitude when it comes to life. My mom will tell you that by the age of three, she envisioned me as the CEO of a large company because of how I took command of everyone around me. I've always had a knack for stepping up and taking the reins in any situation. It's what has propelled me into leadership roles time and time again. With a deep-seated desire to serve, I felt compelled to give back to the community in any way I could. Little did I know, later in life, that our family outreach ministry would become such a defining chapter in my life's story.

Life threw some curveballs that made me reconsider the whole "follow the usual path"–you know, school, degree, career, marriage, the whole nine yards. If I could go back in time, I would ditch the degree altogether and spend that time building myself as an entrepreneur using the resources to build a successful company. Since homeschooling my children, I've made it a point to share all the other possibilities available to them from an early age. This way they know about the endless opportunities, if they get out there and make it happen.

Working for someone else has opened my eyes to see that I'm replaceable, but I'm not replaceable to my family! This principle has been a major life lesson in our family. As an entrepreneurial mother, I want to leave a lasting legacy for my children.

I've never been one to color inside the lines. My mind is always buzzing with creativity, I'm always exploring different paths with the endless possibilities they provide. But here's the kicker: having a gazillion great ideas can make it tough to settle on just one! Despite all these reeling ideas, I ended up taking the conventional route to my end goal as a designer. I went to school, worked hard, and set out to find a job within the field. My plans worked for a while but didn't last, however, God had other plans. Ever felt like your plans went south, but in the end, you saw why they didn't work? Blessings can be in the disguise of closed doors and missed opportunities to get you to the place you are supposed to be. Stick with me and you'll see the blessing!

I started my career with a six-month-old on my hip and freshly married. I had an unrealistic idea of what marriage, parenthood, and a career would require in terms of time, energy, and the learning curve. It was quickly becoming apparent when the demands of the thriving career were more than I bargained for. After being a designer for a few brief years, my health was seriously declining from the stress. On top of the high demands, I had to hustle and jump from job to job to reach my goal. By the time I landed my dream job, I already had several jobs that weren't what I wanted. However, each one of those opportunities led me one step closer to becoming the designer I dreamed of. Not every job or project will be the one you want, but they might be one you need to learn from. This is another principle that gets reiterated within our home. Anything worth doing takes time, dedication, and grit. Remember, Rome wasn't built in a day, and neither will your mom-boss empire.

I had two kids under four by this point and was trading time with them for money. The mom-guilt hit hard, and I was missing their childhood while chasing my dreams. I didn't realize how much of a toll my career was taking on my family, even if it paid well. Even though my boss loved me, and I was very successful at my job, it was too much. Sound familiar? If that's you, I've been there. I know the struggles and guilt about being everything to everyone but somehow losing yourself in the mix while feeling like you're failing your family. I knew that something had to change, but I didn't know how to fix it just yet.

With my stress levels through the roof and trying to be a superwoman, unusual health issues crept in and took center stage in my life. Due to my decisions, my body was heavily taxed to make my dream job happen, and I felt like I was failing miserably. I was juggling the responsibilities of a career woman, wife, and mom; it was proving to be more than my body could keep up with. Burning the candle at both ends, trying to make it all work. I had to make a tough decision. Was it going to be my health or my dream career? I didn't understand the importance of what a mindset shift could do at this moment in my life.

I was a workaholic and so laser-focused on my goals that there was no balance between my family time and work because of the high demands that the job required. I was so dedicated to getting my career successful, that my family was caught in the crossfires of unintentional neglect. During my early years of marriage, I was attempting to raise a family while simultaneously building myself in a highly demanding career. As a young mom and wife, right out of college, you think you can tackle the world, but then reality sets in.

Sometimes it takes drastic measures for God to get our attention; either physical ailments or other life challenges that make us stop and think about what we are doing with our life. Even though going through challenging trials is never easy, what would a testimony be without a test? God had a unique plan, and it was a whirlwind getting to the reality I now live in.

There are so many societal responsibilities that are put on the woman to perform all these duties. Then, we as moms add another layer of stress and expect ourselves to be a superwoman and a high-ranking career professional. All this stress took such a toll on me mentally, emotionally, and physically that my body started to shut down. I ended up getting very sick, which was exacerbated by the overwhelming amount of projects at my job and the demands at home. We couldn't figure out why I was so sick. After dealing with food and environmental allergies most of my life, this illness was beyond all of that. I struggled with major panic and anxiety attacks, weird head pressure, and mood swings; which left me feeling awful all the time. Not only did I have the mental health issues of anxiety and depression, but also physical issues of weight and hair loss. I had a decision to make at that point.

The Shift

The nudge of God during this period was calling me to homeschool and prioritize what I needed to do for myself and my children. It was such a battle in my mind to figure out which way to go. Raising a family is a challenge, especially when there are severe health challenges that impact every aspect of life. However, prioritizing family health during these challenges was way more important than fulfilling any dream. When both parents are working it's hard enough. Then, to add layers of difficulty from unknown health issues, it becomes chaos. We barely had enough hours in the day to get work, school, dinner, and baths finished. To repeat it every day was not only grueling physically, but also mentally. If that's your reality, I feel for you and that's one reason why I knew there had to be a different way.

My faith was severely tested during this time, and I cried out to God, searching for answers. God led me and I trusted his guidance, even if I couldn't see what was next. This was the lowest point in my life, even though I thought it was my ultimate dream. I really had to figure out what God wanted me to do with this situation. I knew if I trusted him, he would take care of it and everything would be under his control.

So many times, we try to take control of the situation when all we really need to do is lay our plans down and pray about it. So that's what I did. After a hard internal struggle, working just a short year, I felt compelled to quit my dream job and homeschool. Not only did I feel God calling me to homeschool, but I heard the whisper to do ministry work alongside it.

My husband, at that point, was not as keen on the idea of me leaving my job because we had planned to both work until we paid our debt off. This shift to the plan was a huge pay cut to our finances. However, I knew if I were to stay in my job, my whole family was going to suffer worse. God had a plan for us, but we had to act on faith. It couldn't go on the way it was and still survive. A better solution was possible; it just required trusting God.

We had to downsize our living space and adjust our monthly expenses so we could live off of one income and there were several sacrifices from both of us to make it happen. This all took place in my life as a test of my family's faith but also so I could share with someone on the other side of their dreams. Despite adversity, you can prosper.

A New Journey

There's something to say about surviving in life versus thriving and there's the challenge of making it from one side of the bridge to the other. It seemed like we were barely surviving, and there was a way we could thrive, but something had to change. We had a long journey ahead of us. We had to walk by faith and not by sight. It wasn't easy. There was still lingering grief I felt from leaving the career that I worked so hard to attain. Not everyone understood my decision to leave. Everyone will not understand yours either, but last time I checked, the call on your heart from God wasn't a conference call needing board members to approve!

There's always going to be highs and lows, and it seemed like a very low point in my life. Regardless, I'm very grateful everything happened, even if it was for reasons I could not see. God has been my greatest supporter and the reason I'm able to keep pushing through all the struggles that have come along with this journey. There was a greater plan unfolding.

Have you experienced brick walls on your journey of entrepreneurship? Sometimes those walls are there to strengthen you as you push through them. Other times, they're placed in your life to make you stop and think. If I didn't go through all the challenges and pitfalls, I wouldn't be able to encourage those going through their own struggles.

After we downsized from our house into a single wide mobile home in an RV park, I started homeschooling the kids. I was so excited to get started on this fresh path, despite struggling with my health. Searching for a solution to heal was still a challenge. I went to a therapy retreat for a week, but unfortunately, it didn't help. It was a great vacation away from the chaos, but not a long-term solution. They still couldn't figure out what was wrong. Thankfully, though, I found a practitioner after that retreat, and they diagnosed my issues were from mold. They gave me a protocol to detox, and I started slowly getting better. After two years of searching and praying, I was on the road to healing. I felt more like myself again and it was a breath of fresh air! This was a turning point in my life. I had a greater outlook on the future and saw the purpose of it all.

The Calling

During this time, we felt God calling our family into ministry work. We were doing some extensive Bible study and felt the call to incorporate ministry work into our lives. This was the turn of a new chapter. This has everything to do with my journey of becoming an entrepreneur because I had to take that leap of faith even when I didn't know how it would work. I had no clue how I was going to accomplish this calling or what it would look like. It took four years before the call laying on my heart would take shape. It lay dormant for so long because it wasn't the time or the place for that idea to come to life. All I knew was that I was supposed to feed God's sheep!

It wasn't until we moved out of state that I even started working on the project. I realized I had set the ball in motion with my mindset years before. So, I set out to create and build something to inspire other families to grow through their trials and support them along the way.

Our mindset is crucial to our outlook on life and the outcome of our efforts. It took a lot for me to stay motivated to keep going. Just like anything in life, we learn to adapt until we can thrive. Having the ability to persevere is crucial when you are forging a new direction. You must walk by faith and have the courage to keep working towards your goal, even when it seems like it's failing.

I've been on this journey for over half a decade and each day I still have to choose how I'm going to respond to obstacles. So how do you stay motivated to work towards those entrepreneurial dreams? Especially when your life is busy with kids and a house to maintain? There are some key elements we will discuss next that affected my personal experience working towards my own goals.

Lessons from Growth

This whole journey has been filled with personal growth. It's only because of the relationships I've built and the mentors that have helped me along the way. I can't stress enough about the importance of working with a coach. This streamlines the process and speeds up the initial learning curve of being an entrepreneur. The most important aspect of entrepreneurial development is taking the time to invest in yourself and heal your inner workings so you can reach those you set out to serve. When you hire a coach, you are not only investing in their expertise, but you are also investing in yourself.

Despite our unique circumstances, there are similarities to the challenges and struggles we all face along the way. When we lean into partnerships and mentors, we have the support we need to succeed. As moms, we need that community of encouragement to keep us on track. We often find ourselves overwhelmed by the never-ending demands of daily life—constantly juggling work, household chores, and caring for our families. It's easy to get caught up in the "Martha spirit" of constant busyness. But I want to challenge you to embrace a different approach, one that prioritizes moments of stillness and connection with your Creator.

Take a cue from Mary and set aside a few minutes each day to simply be present and reflect on the blessings in your life. Whether it's the warmth of the sun on your face or the sweet melody of birdsong. These moments of gratitude can replenish your spirit and provide much-needed clarity in a busy world that can keep you grounded when troubles arise. Through my own entrepreneurial journey, I've learned firsthand that rushing through life is not sustainable or enjoyable. It's essential to take time to refill our cups and nurture our souls if we are to extend a helping hand to others.

Setting realistic priorities, schedules, and goals is key to maintaining balance and avoiding burnout. But how do we achieve our goals while still tending to our families and relationships? It may seem counterintuitive, but carving out just five minutes of quiet solitude each day can make a world of difference. I've used this time to connect with God through prayer and invited Him into all of my plans. His wisdom and guidance far surpass anything I could achieve on my own. It's also important for us to see how God's hand is at work, even during the toughest times. He's empowered me to overcome adversity and keep striving for greater things.

Implementing Your Ideas

So, you have an idea and want to bring it to fruition. What's next? Creating profitable ideas can be overwhelming, and it becomes even more challenging when you have a family to take care of. Coming from experience, it's not impossible, but it takes dedication and patience. Rome wasn't built in a day, and with everything that's worthwhile, it takes time to build it sustainably. Building it alone is also not as effective or efficient, so get a coach and save yourself the hassle. This will give you a better outcome to keep it running long term. When businesses grow too fast, many times they don't have the infrastructure to fulfill the demand.

Whether you are developing a product or a service, don't get discouraged if it takes longer to get it accomplished. It won't be perfect at first and you will constantly be upgrading the content and making changes to improve your business. The best advice to me was to get started before you feel ready to start. If you are waiting to "feel ready," you will never get started. So much of the learning curve won't happen until you get moving and what you need to know is learned along the way.

The most important priority is your job as a mom and everything comes second. However, there are sacrifices that have to be made, and you have to figure out the balance that works best for you and your family. I'm a night owl, but my husband works early mornings. We have scheduled work around naps, school schedules, and bedtimes. His support has been vital to my success. I've experienced scheduling conflicts many times and have canceled or rescheduled because family is the priority.

In my experience, building a business from the ground up with minimal help, while also maintaining a household, was no easy feat. So many times I was on the brink of just giving up. However, the dreams we have need to be made a priority too. The tasks can be completed like a work in progress in the background. The goal is to create something that not only enriches your life but your family's life and the lives that you touch. The short-term sacrifices are worth the long-term goal. Sometimes, that means I've done laundry and cooked at 12 am or written emails before everyone wakes up so I could have the daytime for other scheduled plans. It's all about being flexible, and that can look like two steps forward and one step back. I can't take all the credit. We have very supportive grandparents who have helped with the children and that has been such a blessing!

There's been several days where we had to just forgo the cleaning or sometimes there were hours lost from sleep to get chores done. Of course, it's possible to fill in time gaps during the day but, sometimes it doesn't work that way. You have to just roll with the punches and squeeze in the work where it fits. Maybe that looks like your kids learning to cook dinner while you multitask on your to-do list. If they are still little and nap times are all over the place, you can work on micro tasks and complete them minutes at a time. Sure, it will take longer but, you are accomplishing something versus not getting started at all. Car ride naps were huge when my older children were little; utilize those opportunities! I've joked with my mom friends but I'm serious about building out a laptop and phone holder for my car to turn it into a mobile office since I'm always carting children everywhere!

Staying organized is a huge issue at our house. I have had to work so hard to keep everything together and manageable. If that's you, take heart. It will be clean and quiet soon enough, so embrace the mess, and just work with what you've got! I'm not just talking about myself struggling with clutter, it's my whole family. When your space is constantly getting disorganized, it's hard to keep your thoughts straight. I'm not the first person you've heard say this, but I have noticed that when my space is orderly, I can think clearly.

Even if you can't get the entire house the way you want it organized, at least clear a section of your countertop or a shelf just for your business things. When I started writing ideas down for projects in various notebooks and journals, they were scattered throughout the house and I wasted so much time searching. I've ditched a lot of the notebooks and now use my phone notepad to keep all my notes. It's been the best choice to switch from paper because I can search for words and it finds my notes for me, score! However, putting plans on paper has more power than you think, and keeping ideas organized will keep you on track and motivated to continue working.

Mindset Makes a Difference

Our words have the power to lift us up or tear us down. What we write has even more influence than our spoken words. Writing your plans out first and then putting those ideas up where you will see them daily can keep you inspired to continue to work towards those goals. The only bad plans are the ones that you aren't willing to make. This has been a huge part of the success I've had.

Not only have I prayed about these plans and projects but, I've also written them down more than once and hung them on my bedroom door where I can see them along with my prayer board. This is where a vision board can help make these plans easier to keep track of, but also as inspiration. Even just writing down bullet points and being able to look at them daily will make a vast difference. Our brain sees them as more concrete and believable than just an idea in our head when we write it down.

Plans have to shift and adjust, and you will have plenty of setbacks in life but, every day something can get done, whether it's moving towards your goals an inch or a mile. I will say a huge thanks to my supportive husband, family, and friends. They keep me accountable for my goals. It makes a tremendous difference when you have a support system to lean on! If you don't have the support or you are trying to create something privately until it's complete, take heart; you will succeed if you don't quit. It might take several renditions before you find the direction you want to take, but eventually, you will find what works. Remember, it's not a cakewalk; more like a volcano walk without shoes! But you can walk through the fire and come out stronger than ever.

When you are doing something you love and have a passion for it, the time, energy, and effort you spend will make it more enjoyable. You will feel like the investment you are putting in is worth the sacrifice involved. Remember this: if you are creating something that fulfills your purpose, how much better can you serve by feeling like your efforts are making a difference?

I'm in the mindset that serving your family needs to come first; however, there is something to be said about family community service. Yes, being a wife and mother are the most important jobs you could ever have. But, if God puts a desire in your heart to do something, He will make a way for it to happen. He gives us the strength to make a way when it seems like there is no way.

If you have that desire and can't seem to get it started, maybe it's not the right time yet. Sometimes we want to jump ahead of the plans God has for us. But that doesn't mean it isn't supposed to happen. When I finally got started with my nonprofit, it had been over four years since

I got the idea to do a family outreach ministry. If you feel like it's impossible to build what you are trying to start, get relationships built first. Start talking about it and share your ideas with your closest friends. You can then leverage your network and find people who can help you build your vision. Remember, relationships are one of the primary keys to getting an idea to fruition. Yes, you could build a business on your own, but for it to be sustainable, collaboration with key people involved will help you make it happen. This also allows you to have a better balance between your entrepreneurial journey and your family responsibilities.

When you're rooted in the source of pure love, your capacity to make a meaningful impact in the world becomes limitless. You'll start a ripple effect that extends far beyond what you can imagine, touching the lives of others in profound ways. So, despite life's challenges and uncertainties, don't be afraid to pursue your dreams with boldness and determination. Stay organized, write out your goals and vision, and build those relationships to make it all happen. Remember, your story is still unfolding, and the next chapter could hold transformative possibilities beyond your wildest dreams.

We have gone through several phases of my experience. I hope it has helped you gain some wisdom to make decisions for your own journey. I'm happy to help you towards your goals! I have helped several moms find clarity about their calling and helped them see the possibilities and the capabilities they have right before them. Remember, prioritize your family but also get started with something and slowly build it up in the background and you will be well on your way to reaching your goals of success.

Toks Omowunmi Olunloyo

Purple Patch Cereals
Mom Coach | Food Business Mentor | Speaker

https://www.linkedin.com/in/toks-omowunmi-olunloyo-58363110
https://www.facebook.com/OmowunmiOlunloyo/
https://www.instagram.com/omowunmi_toks/
www.purplepatchcereals.co.uk
https://linktr.ee/toksolunloyo

Omowunmi Olunloyo, known as Toks, is a multifaceted professional with over a decade of experience as a busy working mother coach, food technologist, bestselling author, film producer, and speaker. She has graced the airwaves of Reconcilers Radio, Hope FM, and Premier Christian Radio and received prestigious accolades like the Courageous Award. As the Owner of Purple Patch Cereals, an award-winning breakfast cereal brand, she fulfils her dream of providing healthy food for health-conscious families. Toks also heads Peacock Omowunmi Production, releasing her debut movie "Hustle" to acclaim. Her journey from personal struggles to empowerment drives her mission to help women especially mothers find purpose and fulfilment, highlighted in her international bestselling books, The Purpose Driven Lady magazine, and Motherhood Aid CIC. Respected for her loyalty and inspiration, Toks empowers busy working mothers to thrive in every aspect of life.

BALANCING THE DEMANDS OF MOTHERHOOD AND ENTREPRENEURSHIP: A GUIDE TO THRIVING AS A MOMPRENEUR

By Toks Omowunmi Olunloyo

Introduction

Motherhood and entrepreneurship—two distinct roles that often intertwine, creating a delicate balancing act for women just like you and me around the world. In the pursuit of accomplishing dreams and aspirations, many mothers must juggle the demands of running a business and caring for a family. This chapter serves as a guide for women to succeed as mothers and entrepreneurs, providing practical tips, inspiring stories, and valuable insights to navigate the challenges and joys of this unique journey.

A Rough Road

Life was hard for me. Meeting the demands of being both a mother and an entrepreneur was a struggle. That was then. This is now.

Now I am living my best life, filled with joy, and making an impact.

"Motherhood teaches us to love unconditionally, and entrepreneurship teaches us to dream fearlessly." - Sheryl Sandberg

The Beginning

One of my greatest challenges was accepting that I was enough and that good would come out of my life. I was a people pleaser, always trying to be somebody that I was not.

This part of my life was a very dark moment; I did not think I would amount to anything. I did not love myself, and I certainly did not think that I was beautiful. To think I would be married was dream talk, not even to mention being a mother and running multiple businesses.

I gave up my purpose for fear of rejection, abandonment, and loneliness. I struggled with low self-esteem and fitting in the crowd. I could not see past my shortcomings; I felt like a loser. Every aspect of my life was impacted, so I was disrespected, separated, and abused. I was called all kinds of names under the sun, and my self-worth was next to none.

Despite the various challenges I faced growing up, I still had a fight in me. I did not give up. I remember my first serious relationship that I thought would lead to marriage ending abruptly after two and a half years without any reason. You cannot begin to imagine the heartbreak I felt - another rejection that I did not understand. My self-esteem was knocked back, and I began to struggle again; it was like a crazy figure-eight circle. But somehow, love found me again. I entered another relationship that led to marriage in September 2005. 19 years later with three amazing children, I have a lot to be thankful for. The stone that the builder has rejected has become a cornerstone.

I often pinch myself from time to time for the life that I am currently living. I still ask myself, am I dreaming? Of course, I know the answer, this is no dream; I am well aware, living a life on purpose.

I launched a weekend retreat program for women where they learn to rest and receive and started a coaching business for mothers where I help them to overcome stress and overwhelm so that they can find a place, position, and purpose that will allow them to create their reality. I help people who enjoy making food to turn their love for cooking into a profitable food business, published my own magazine "The Purpose Driven Lady" in 2016, and guess who was the cover girl four times in a row? Yours truly. I have published three books and co-authors in two anthologies, making five books to date, and here I am co-authoring with She Rises Studio, sharing a message of hope and possibility.

That is just the beginning. I was elected President of DSAP Set 36 in 2022 where one of my major accomplishments was raising close to half a million naira for the organisation. I produced a movie named "Hustle" that is currently showing on Amazon Prime after its release in Nigeria and the UK in 2023. I registered my CIC in 2023, "Motherhood Aid," which supports women, especially mothers, to thrive and enjoy the motherhood experience. I was appointed Zonal Coordinator for APC Professional Women's Council in 2023. I have anchored several online and offline events such as book launches, birthday celebrations, wedding receptions, and conferences, and acted as a TV host. I have spoken on different platforms on topics supporting motherhood, childhood, and womanhood.

I am also the owner of the award-winning breakfast cereal company called "Purple Patch Cereals." With 10 products in the range from granola and muesli to porridge, we supply farm shops with premium, homemade cereals and also have an online presence that is growing.

Doors are open to me because I dared to believe that just maybe I am that special, unique, and different, and that is absolutely fine. I simply believed that I could, and I did. I am now a minister of enjoyment. I rest and receive.

But how did I get here? How was I able to balance the demands of motherhood and entrepreneurship? How did I become the best version of myself living life on my terms? Let me share the steps I took that brought about this amazing transformation that you see today.

Steps to change

Sick and tired of being sick and tired, I had to take drastic action to improve the quality of life I was living. I knew I was made for more, even though I did not know how it could happen.

After attending a women's conference in Chicago, I had a light bulb moment, and for some reason, I could see clearly. It was as if the scales in my eyes fell off. For the first time after several years of living a mediocrity kind of life, I was free, and free I was indeed.

During this awareness period of my life, I found journaling and began to write more frequently. I wrote every day about everything that rocked my world, this is an extract from it:

"Do not faint, your time for reward is here keep at it." This was spoken to me in January 2013 by one of my mentors. I received the word but did not see how that could happen. I believed in the faith he had in the words he said to me.

1. So, journalling was a key part of balancing the demands of motherhood and entrepreneurship.

Fuelled by a passion to serve and commitment to make a difference, I renewed my mind. I did this by listening to messages that were uplifting and gave me hope, and gradually, over time, I was able to be, do, and have effortlessly. That is how my story began to change. My favourite book reminded me that as I think in my heart so am I. I started to think happy thoughts so that my actions were powerful, pleasant, and positive.

I took responsibility for my actions. I began to consciously watch what I allowed to enter my life. I protected my space jealously. I chose to operate by faith. I realised that unless I listened, faith would not come. I was committed to my faith despite everything trying to stop me from believing. Saying and doing is a lifestyle of a believer, I was told, so I spoke. I speak to myself a lot; my friends can testify to this.

My life is a demonstration of the proof that it is possible. I began to see a lot of value in myself. From no hope to having hope, and this hope translates to faith. I received the revelation in the words I heard, and it made it easy to speak. It is about believing, ladies, that your action dictates your faith.

Yes, I felt stuck, but I was ready to live in integrity with my own values, not somebody else's. Not my friends', not even society's; I acted despite the fear I felt.

2. This is one of the ways I balanced the demands of motherhood and entrepreneurship that transformed my life.

I made a decision to embrace the mompreneurial spirit while prioritising my family values. I decided to love myself, to accept that I was good enough and that I was beautiful. Love is such a powerful force. Then, I told a few people about my new decision. I saw myself achieving my decision and I used a vision board to bring it to life. I created confessions, or affirmations as some like to call them, which I still declare daily. I was very intentional about setting goals for my family and business that were realistic so that they could be achieved within the given time limit. Managing time effectively is vital to achieving a sense of balance and fulfilment as a mompreneur.

As I achieved my goal by taking little, actionable steps, I rewarded myself. This did something to my mind. I believed in myself more, and it helped to reaffirm and reinforce my behaviour. For you to have faith, you must hear and believe. I experienced the best when I acted out my faith. It is important to know that success in business does not have to come at the expense of family life. In fact, there is a lot of common ground in both areas. I am talking about transferable skills. It is about finding harmony between the two and understanding that they can complement each other.

I found purpose and passion as a mother and entrepreneur because of the deep sense of fulfilment I got from accomplishing two dreams. I am very grateful for the capacity and opportunity to be able to do this.

When self-doubt or impostor syndrome showed their ugly heads, I dealt with them by recognising and acknowledging those feelings. It helped me to understand that it is part of the entrepreneurial journey.

I focussed on my strengths and delegated my weaknesses when I did not have the capacity to deal with those situations. Choosing the right people in my circle supported and boosted my confidence, especially during difficult times. I practiced self-care and prioritised personal well-being because it is essential for maintaining energy and focus on both my business and family life

By embracing the mompreneurial mindset, I applied my values of motherhood (such as being nurturing, having patience, and showing empathy) to the business world. It is about viewing challenges as opportunities for growth and setbacks as lessons to be learned from. One of my favourite quotes says, "In life, there is no failure, you either learn or you win."

3. Making a decision to embrace the mompreneurial spirit is one of the secret sauces to balancing the demands of motherhood and entrepreneurship.

Navigating the challenges of being a mother and entrepreneur is very important in getting better results in life. If not it can lead to overwhelm, stress, and frustration. I settled three core areas that allowed me to thrive as a mompreneur.

a. Establishing boundaries
b. Dealt with mom-guilt
c. Time management

Establishing boundaries: the importance of having boundaries cannot be overemphasized. To have meaningful results that produce impact, boundaries must be set to protect family time from business time. This means clear and simple instructions must be in place describing how business-related activities will be managed that will not impact the family. From hours of operation to how to respond to out-of-office matters (including how to communicate these to all stakeholders involved). Learning how to say no will make your life easier, especially for activities that can be delegated or that do not have any impact on your business. The benefits are plenty including but not limited to avoiding burnout, maintaining your energy, and focusing on an allocated task that matters.

Dealing with mom-guilt: Some moms in business often feel guilty because they are giving time to their business instead of being with their children 100%. I want to say, it is important that you know it is normal to feel torn between both responsibilities; there is nothing wrong with you. One of the ways to deal with mom-guilt is to find ways to involve your family in your business. Giving them certain tasks will make them feel as if they are part of the business and allow them to buy into the vision of your business. It will promote a supportive family environment and create unity and a shared sense of purpose. Building a network of family and friends who understand and support the demands of both parenting and business ownership is crucial. Establishing open communication and mutual respect fosters a positive, nurturing environment where everyone feels valued and appreciated.

Time management: Managing time is essential for everyone, especially a mother in business. To thrive, you have to be a good time manager; this can be achieved by implementing strategies that will optimise productivity in the home and business. Strategies like using a calendar, planner, and time tracking devices to schedule tasks and allocate the correct time. I always say that what does not get scheduled, does not get done. Scheduled = Will Get Done. Another way to manage time effectively is to prioritise tasks based on urgency and importance. Doing this will help promote a healthy work-life balance and get better results at home and in business.

4. Navigating the challenges of being a mother and entrepreneur by establishing boundaries, dealing with mom-guilt, and effective time management allowed me to balance the demands of motherhood and entrepreneurship.

In closing, as a mother in business, it is important that you are in a supportive environment with like-minded mothers just like you. Like the popular quote says, "Birds of the same feathers flock together." Being in such company fosters connection, support, inspiration, and collaboration. It allows you to share insights, resources, and experiences, as well as address challenges and celebrate successes. The major benefit of building a network of like-minded mothers in business is the community spirit; you can always find encouragement and motivation when you need it.

In the community, there are opportunities for mentorship and guidance for running a successful business. Being mentored by experienced mompreneurs is helpful for personal and professional growth, especially mentors who have successfully cracked the code of winning at home and in business. This is a great chance to learn from them to avoid common errors and accelerate the journey toward success. By leveraging the wisdom and expertise of a seasoned mompreneur, you can gain confidence and clarity in your entrepreneurial pursuits.

5. Having a supportive community where mentoring and guidance are available will give you the opportunity to balance the demands of motherhood and entrepreneurship.

As we continue to embrace the dual roles of motherhood and entrepreneurship, I want to remind you that you can thrive in both your personal and professional lives. This chapter serves as a beacon

of inspiration and empowerment for mompreneurs everywhere, guiding you on your journey to success and fulfilment.

Remember that you are capable, you are resilient, and you are unstoppable. Let us embrace each challenge as an opportunity for growth and each setback as a stepping stone to success. Together, we can redefine what it means to be a mompreneur and pave the way for future generations of women to pursue their entrepreneurial dreams while nurturing their families.

So, to all the mompreneurs out there, I say: keep dreaming, keep striving, and keep shining your light. The world needs your unique talents and perspectives now more than ever. Let us continue to embrace the mompreneurial spirit and make our mark on the world, one courageous step at a time.

Final words

In closing, in the words of the former First Lady of America Michelle Obama in her final, official, emotional farewell speech, for you reading right now, "Know that you are enough." Do not ever let anyone make you feel like you do not matter or that you do not have a place, position, or purpose because you do. And you have a right to be exactly who you are.

I want all women to know that they matter and that they belong, so do not be afraid. Do you hear me?

Women, do not be afraid. Be focused, be determined. Be hopeful. Be empowered. Empower yourselves with a good education, then get out there and use that knowledge to build an environment, a community, and a society worthy of your boundless promise. Lead by example with hope, never fear. And know that I'll be with you, rooting for you, and working to support you for the rest of my life. And that is true. I know this is true for every co-author who is in this amazing book who gets up every day and works their heart out to lift up other women.

I am so grateful to all of you for your passion, sense of purpose, and your dedication. And I can think of no better way to end my story than celebrating you for taking the bold step to transform your life. So, I want to close by saying thank you. Thank you for believing in yourself enough to invest in your education, personal development, and growth. Being a co-author in the "Becoming An Unstoppable Woman: Mompreneur" series is one of the greatest honours of my life, and I hope I have inspired you and shined a torch of light and hope on you.

JOIN THE MOVEMENT!
#BAUW

Becoming An Unstoppable Woman
With She Rises Studios

She Rises Studios was founded by Hanna Olivas and Adriana Luna Carlos, the mother-daughter duo, in mid-2020 as they saw a need to help empower women worldwide. They are the podcast hosts of the *She Rises Studios Podcast* and Amazon best-selling authors and motivational speakers who travel the world. Hanna and Adriana are the movement creators of #BAUW - Becoming An Unstoppable Woman: The movement has been created to universally impact women of all ages, at whatever stage of life, to overcome insecurities, and adversities, and develop an unstoppable mindset. She Rises Studios educates, celebrates, and empowers women globally.

Looking to Join Us in our Next Anthology or Publish YOUR Own?

She Rises Studios Publishing offers full-service publishing, marketing, book tour, and campaign services. For more information, contact info@sherisesstudios.com

We are always looking for women who want to share their stories and expertise and feature their businesses on our podcasts, in our books, and in our magazines.

SEE WHAT WE DO

OUR PODCAST

OUR BOOKS

OUR SERVICES

Be featured in the Becoming An Unstoppable Woman magazine, published in 13 countries and sold in all major retailers. Get the visibility you need to LEVEL UP in your business!

Have your own TV show streamed across major platforms like Roku TV, Amazon Fire Stick, Apple TV and more!

Learn to leverage your expertise. Build your online presence and grow your audience with FENIX TV.
https://fenixtv.sherisesstudios.com/

Visit www.SheRisesStudios.com to see how YOU can join the #BAUW movement and help your community to achieve the UNSTOPPABLE mindset.

Have you checked out the *She Rises Studios Podcast?*

Find us on all MAJOR platforms: Spotify, IHeartRadio, Apple Podcasts, Google Podcasts, etc.

Looking to become a sponsor or build a partnership?

Email us at info@sherisesstudios.com